Burroughs

&

Scotland

Dethroning the Ancients: The Commitment of Exile

by Chris Kelso

(Illustrations by Shane Swank)

A Beatdom Books Publication

Published by Beatdom Books

Cover Design: Matthew Revert

View the publisher's website:
www.books.beatdom.com

Printed in the United Kingdom
First Print Edition
ISBN 978-0-9934099-7-4

For Graham Masterton, Alex Neish, and Graham Rae.

Thanks to David S. Wills, Shane Swank, Oliver Harris, Eva Kowalska, Jed Birmingham, Barry Miles, Ewan Morrison, Graham Rae, James Grauerholz, Hal Duncan, Graham Masterton, Ken MacLeod, Preston Grassmann, Jimme O'Neil, Stewart Home, James Pennington, Gillian Tasker, Ted Morgan, Steve Finbow, Andrew Gallix, Barry Graham, Jim Steel.

Praise for the Author

"Kelso is a fearless and accomplished prose stylist."

– Ray Nessly, *Literary Orphans*

"Chris Kelso writes in a style of broken glass and razor blades, barbed wire and gasoline. Stitching together prose, poetry, drama, and graphic novel in a Frankenstein aesthetic..."

– John Langan, *The Wide, Carnivorous Sky and Other Monstrous Geographies*

"I think Kelso is a major talent and you'll hear more about him as time goes by. However, his work is not for the squeamish. His work is transgressive, erudite, shocking."

– Mary Turzillo, NEBULA winner

"Just when you're wondering if there are actually still writers out there who still feel and live their ideas out on the page, I come across a writer like Kelso, and suddenly the future feels a lot more optimistic. One calls to mind Burroughs, and Trocchi's more verbose offerings - whilst remaining uniquely himself, in a writer as young as he is, is a very encouraging sign: one of maturity that belies his youth. I look forward to reading more from him in the near future."

— Andrew Raymond Drennan, *The Immaculate Heart*

"Someday soon people will be naming him as one of their own influences."

— ***INTERZONE* magazine**

"Sparky, modern, avant-garde but accessible, Chris Kelso's book is reminiscent of the most successful literary experimentation of the sixties and seventies, the sort of work that was published in the later New Worlds, but it's also thoroughly contemporary, intimately engaged with modern life as it is right now. Kelso steams with talent and dark wit and his blend of anarchy with precision is refreshing, inspiring and utterly entertaining..."

— **Rhys Hughes, *Mister Gum***

"Whether he's writing about a fictionalized William S. Burroughs, Time Detectives, or Aliens Chris Kelso aims at the interstices or the Interzones because he understands that these are the people and spaces that define modern life – Kelso is also always funny and twisted."

— **Douglas Lain**

Contents

Humans have a need to
principally express
abstractions algorithmicall

The behavior of human
beings set against the socia
backdrop tends to make such
rules precise yet nearly al
that you percieve quickly
gets lost in an artificial
paradigm.

In binary practice, when
understanding deviates from
the visual world I am
especially adept at dealing
in technology.

Shooting up Scotland

by Graham Rae

"That Bards are second-sighted is nae joke
And ken the lingo of the sp'ritual folk
Fays, Spunkies, Kelpies, a' they can explain them
And ev'n the very deils they brawly ken them"
- Robert Burns, *The Brigs of Ayr*

In the late fifties and early sixties, long before *Trainspotting* was a rancid twinkle in Scottish druggie literature's bloodshot eye, American gentleman junkie William Seward Burroughs had already slid his novel needle *Naked Lunch* under Scotland's moribund literary flesh, shooting it up with his diseased, scatological, hilarious visions.

It's safe to say that our then-parochial national literature was never quite the same again, recoiling from Burroughs' druggie homosexual confrontational words in fear and loathing and confusion. But there was also interest in what the man was doing with his words, and he found his supporters on these shores as well. As expertly delineated in these pages by Burroughs aficionado, Chris Kelso, the gutter-stuttering Midwestern outcast's *danse macabre* visions were the *cause célèbre* of the 1962 International Writers Conference in Edinburgh. Scottish junkie *enfant terrible* writer Alex Trocchi and other "cosmopolitan scum" (as Hugh MacDiarmid humorously termed Trocchi) took sides against the literary old guard, the creak-kneed purveyors of frail kailyard tales, the rustic jiggers, the never-movers-and-shakers. They're the same ones who would have taken a sort of hypocritical pride in the time Edgar Allan Poe spent as a child in Scotland, and the gothic effect it had on his adult writing. Yet when faced with a modern manifestation of dark haunted brilliance, they cowered in aw-fuck-here-comes-the-meteor Jurassic idiocy.

But if the ancient hissyfit regime had taken the time to remove their thistle-scored heads from their wrinkled bahookies, they might well have had much more in common with the prophetic visceral neon mutterings of the American junkie *brujo* in a heroin trance than at first might have seemed possible. Scotland is not a young land; it is old and dirty and tired. The still-contested soil here is soaked in blood and pain and horror, and centuries of internecine clan carnage – and fighting the still-colonising English – have rendered the Scottish psyche very dark and cynical indeed.

Burroughs's spectral secret agent provocateur entrance into the Scottish literary scene should really have come as no surprise to the country's writers. He was a walking, talking archetype, after all. His coming had been forebodingly foretold in Scottish novels like *The Private Memoirs and Confessions of a Justified Sinner* (James Hogg, 1824) and *Strange Case of Dr Jekyll and Mr Hyde* (Robert Louis Stevenson, 1886). He was the Divided Man, dark and light, the Midwestern patrician background escapee with the ironically sober, sombre demeanour of a mortician. He was a suit-clad, ostensibly upstanding man, with all sorts of deviant tendencies lurking barely repressed under the bland, personable, cool façade. Maybe that instant dichotomous familiarity was what scared some of the Scots writers who reacted so violently to him, raging against the coming of the threatening foreign literary dark.

This country had the world's first literate society, as the church had Scotland educated so we were able to read the Bible. One person who would have found this aspect of Scottish society to be praiseworthy would have been Dr. James Wideman Lee (1849-1919), a pastor, writer, and world traveller. He was the grandfaither of William S. Burroughs on his mother Laura Hammond Lee's side, and it's from the matrilineal side of the family that William got his writing talent. In 1920, Lee published a book entitled *The Geography of Genius*, about the effects of environment on genius and its global expression, in the arts or in general culture. On p.128, Lee visits Scotland, more specifically Ayr, and pontificates approvingly on Robert Burns, the Scottish Bard, and his surroundings:

"One feels, in the Burns country, as if there had been

a subtle giving off of the poet's interior being, a passing of its essence into its immediate surroundings, a process which might be compared to the outrush of electrons from an atom of radium."

In a way, this is not too far from Burroughs's own musings on how he believed he was possessed by what he termed "the Ugly Spirit," though here it is a beautiful poetic spirit possessing a living writer's immediate surroundings. You very much doubt, though, whether the indignant Scottish mid-century literary cognoscenti, brows gathering like a storm, nursing their wrath to keep it warm, knew anything about this earlier American tribute to Scottish poetry by the 1962 Edinburgh International Book Festival *bête noire*'s grandfaither. They might also have gotten their knickers in a twist if they had found out that Burroughs had, hilariously, misidentified Edinburgh as being in England in *Naked Lunch*, a mistake James Lee would probably never have made.

Whatever William S. Burroughs was possessed by, it was, in part, genius, and the death-rattle comedy in his work fits the Scottish psyche like a twisted glove. Comics like Frankie Boyle tell disgusting home truths that their love-to-be-shocked audiences wolf down. Burroughs' charnel house comedy came from upper-middle-class repression and personal pain, and these are two things that the Scots understand right down to our rain-loving, joyously sorrowful marrow.

It's the reason why we love sick adult comedians like the Australian Jim Jefferies, or even the closeted homosexual black American comic Rudy Ray Moore, whose underground raps like "Bulldaggers" ("A punk got drunk and shit in the lunch!") come off like a rhyming version of *Naked Lunch*. We're twisted fuckers in Scotland, and, like black Americans, we like our comedy brutally bulldag-biting down to the bone and beyond. Which is why the disgusting, ultra-cerebral hilarity of *Naked Lunch* or "Roosevelt After Inauguration" resonates so deeply with us.

This used to be a church-controlled, Calvinistic, sexually repressed, macho, violent, dark-minded, witch-burning country, and our fractured laughter is screaming who-fucking-cares promises of survival into the yawning maw of the void. In a once-superstitious nation where the aforementioned Rabbie Burns could write a Devil-chased, anti-chaste masterpiece like "Tam o' Shanter," and the modern Scottish musician-poet Gerry Cinnamon can sing "I got different voices inside my head/I got plenty of demons under my bed/but I don't get scared cos I'm already dead," then the self-damning, self-damaging actions of a pained genius like Burroughs clearly resonate and reverberate. We recognise the independent-minded, anarchaotic, anti-authoritarian doomed and damned when we see them, sense in them our own senseless self-destructive habits, and the addition of chemicals only adds opiate fuel to the Celtic psyche-fire. We have been reading since before anycunt, we love words and poetry, with warrior-poet archetypes roaring up for acknowledgement from the brutal bloody chestbeater past. William S. Burroughs speaks to the Scots in a damned demented voice like one that would have been used by his pastor grandfaither, a voice of fire and brimstone and hot sick Book of Revelations image-madness, an insane howling pastor chased by his own demons 'round the globe. The fact he and his friends used to act out routines from the work fits perfectly. Scotland is a country of rough religious damnation oral tradition, and the pathological utterances and horrifying internal visions of the twentieth century high priest of harmful matter make our internal compass hit true north. And always will. This book is a testament to that.

Enjoy.

Introduction

The Broken Boy

I love my town, even if it doesn't love me back. I often wonder how Burroughs would have observed it. Would it have been a sympathetic take? Perhaps he saw Scotland as an old body. The Scots are the aging cells that have become larger and less able to divide and multiply. When they look at you it's all pigments and fatty lipids. Weary eyes buried beneath clumps of abnormal tissue. These cells have been sick for the longest time. Individually they are harmless but when conglomerated they seek to inhibit normal control of the host and can become tumorous. This is not the fault of the cell. It is merely fulfilling its inevitable function at the behest of a naturally-occurring pathogen. Fate. But the body, the old town that lumbers forth in immortal quietude, becomes restless. Pain becomes a normal sensation. It starts to show the scars of a warring inner-system. The wounds of betrayal. But the people provide structure for the town-body, take in nutrients from food and convert those into energy. Without the people, even in their diseased state, the town would cease to exist. Maybe Burroughs would have been more sympathetic. I don't know. What I do know is that a silent scream will send us all to bed tonight and Burroughs shares our nightmares. Not even Hassan-i Sabbah can do it without apomorphine.

Having successfully willed some kind of astral-migration from the dim-shores of Cumnock to the less-dim-shores of Kilmarnock, I was inclined to believe myself in possession of supernatural powers from an early age. You see, it was a frequent dream of mine to exchange my small-town backwater for big-town living. The dead never really died in these provincial places, and Cumnock kept its corpses vertical for years, even after the mind had ceased neural activity. One need only take a walk past my old flat with adjoined graveyard to see this phenomenon in effect. One look out the window gave you unforgettable images of abject horror – adolescent cadavers bouncing on the bonnet of your car, a sallow-skinned witch-cum-drug addict burning kittens alive in industrial oil drums, and freshly exhumed retirees searching for coins of a fictional romantic past. These were my stock. My genealogy of eternal misery. It didn't help that I'd been brought up to support the rival football team.

While the Kelsos lived in Cumnock for a long time and strobalised heartily for almost a generation. The family dynasty actually traced its origins to the neighbouring town of Auchinleck. The football team in question was Talbot FC, a surprisingly successful and enigmatic little institution. I inherited this as well. At least this inheritance brought with it a legacy of achievement. My attachment to Cumnock was tenuous at best, for Allah's sake. I always felt like an outsider – which, to be fair, had been exacerbated because of an incident that occurred on the final day of primary school before the Easter holiday. I had recently been lambasted for kissing my male friend on the cheek during a game of Truth or Dare (a transgression that saw me socially exiled for the entirety of the Easter break and subsequent remainder of my final year at Cumnock Primary School). I was scolded for being gay by children and adults alike. One jaunt round Sainsbury's with my mum and dad comes to mind. A walk down the tinned food aisle soon turned into a game of cat and mouse when a group of students from my year caught sight of my timid beta frame and went to extraordinary lengths to publicly gay-bash me. Ironically, I was not gay and am still not gay. At the time this was not a place of fairness or irony or self-awareness or indeed progressive thought. Even the teachers were disgusted by this innocuous act of comradery. I was transgressive at eleven. I was a Broken Boy.

But Kilmarnock was different. It promised much more. This was a place my parents took me to on weekends, a town of cobbled streets and grand toyshops. A bustling grey-scape of concrete multi-story carparks and brutalist council conapts. *Ballardian* is the word. By the roadside, aborted sentinels with Edwardian baroque frontage loomed – buildings where poltergeists of a certain brogue and candour roamed the boards at their own discretion, haunting the collective consciousness of the Kilmarnock ideal. A high street full of commerce and culture – and, yes, a *real* football team who played in the nation's top league. I think about Hasbro toy lines and falling in love with science fiction and horror because in Kilmarnock these tastes were somewhat facilitated by the chain store.

You can imagine my elation when my mother completed her PhD and immediately got a job working for Vaskutek, a medical device company based in Glasgow, which meant we had to move somewhere closer. Kilmarnock was top of the list. Little did I know I was exchanging one Bauhausian wet dream for another.

My superpowers have dwindled in later life. I find myself living in a functionalist box amidst a divided community set in a large cluster of buildings called Onthank. I move into Morven Avenue, kitschily redubbed "Morphine Avenue," and observe the silent streets and steel-shuttered windows. Burroughs, Huncke, and the 1940s Times Square hustler community would have been happy here. The air becomes redolent of Danang after a Daisy Cutter blitzing. Tall grass. An underlying threat of violence. Smoke hanging in the nostril. The echo of vague and distant screams. A sense that there is a generation of

Broken Boys who need help more than they need a fix. You know, this "Onthank" is dreamily similar to the purgatorial wilderness Duncan Thaw finds himself awakened to in Alasdair Gray's opus, *Lanark*. "Unthank" has an almanac "based on sunlight, but only administrators use it. The majority have forgotten the sun." Onthank is a borough of the machine aesthetic, where people have given up, forgotten the sun – a quarter that is soon to be scrapped by the high-heed-yins because all town industry has died and a toxic feeling of melancholy has pervaded every strip of brick and plaster the place has to offer. But it survives because the people will it to live.

A man, late-30s, wearing Kappa popper trackies and Burberry cap emerges from a two-row house with a haunted, disenfranchised expression on his face that would make Orwell blush. A moveable void. Another Broken Boy. Breaking the silence terrifies me. I become aware of lactic acid in my calves and hope I don't need to run. I feel heavy, useless. Like a weak animal I'm ready to lay on my back and present my belly to the oncoming predator. Because this fella could kill me with his determined sadness alone. He sucks me into his gaze the way Nietzsche teases the abyss. The young gunslinger stops on the third step of his stoop, sneers. His hand rummaging in his pockets, either brazenly juggling his testicles, pocket-dialing for the squad (He's going to meet *Clem*, Carl, and Joselito to pick up a pound of Black Meat anyway), or simply searching for a concealed weapon. Fingers crossed for option number one.

There is no dragonhide affliction like Duncan Thaw has to deal with but the welts of our loss are evident for all to see. We inherit this grief like we inherit our football team loyalties. Mourning the lost glory days of Massie-Ferguson, Andrew Barclay & Sons, and the Johnnie Walker Hill Street plant is a joy we will never surrender. The people wear their suits of pain with pride. The Ugly Spirit can rest comfortable and safe. I do too. In the wake of the American Civil War, the cotton market declined but this did bring about the prevalence of steam power as the hot new industry. The economy of Kilmarnock was at its peak with the arrival of heavy engineering in the mid-19th century. The Kilmarnock to Troon plateway had been built to transport coal from mining enclaves around the town to coastal shipping venues. The plateway evolved and soon the town had the prestigious honour of being the first train service to carry passengers. I can see Broken Boys and Transgressive Men walking towards me who would have been flourishing labourers back in the day, shawl makers and calico-printers. Now something has balled their eyes from the sockets and replaced them with watery orbs of unseeing insect indifference. What would be the point in seeing when everything you liked looking at had been eviscerated, never to return? What's the point in seeing what you can't love? When you remove the capacity for love you remove the most vital component of a developing organism. Growth stops. Where does perspective go when you barely live in this reality? Hanging on the wall of the Goldberry pub is an article written by Hugh McIlvanney:

"The All-Scottish Deanxietised Man." McIlvanney wrote about these people but he impregnated them with a hard-edged charm. Towards the end, even he couldn't ignore the way his town was headed: "It is disturbing to visit your hometown and find it disappearing up its own planning permission."

The armchair literati will offer you an exegesis of the fabled *Kilmarnock Edition*, the first collection of work by Scottish poet Robert Burns. It's a favourite past-time of ours to gloat about that to which we have no formal connection and have made no contribution. More than anything, we love to wax lyrical about our connection to Burns. The fetishisation of this poet is an affliction befouling many a Kilmarnock local. Walk into a pub – the Goldberry, for example, or the Charleston – and speak to a man over 50 and with vicarious pride he will regale you with a detailed story of the *Kilmarnock Edition*. It's our link to the wider world – but then Cumnock has Carmen Ejogo[1] and the helicopter scene from *Mission: Impossible* to boast about. We have our Nobel Prize winners and have made our contributions to science and the arts, but Burns is a precious commodity. He elevates the Broken Boy to the status of a poet. Kind of. Really, we want to let Burns take us to bed and treat us like one of his floozies. All's forgiven, Rabbie. Separate the art from the artist and all

1 Carmen Ejogo is a Hollywood actress who spent her formative years in Cumnock.

that.

The gunslinger moves to the final step of his stoop. We've been staring at each other for several seconds. He smiles, yanks the fabric of his trackie-bottoms and reveals the deformed turkey of his cock and balls. Low-hanging fruit.

I wander through the maze of council houses and emerge from the anus of the scheme intact. These are routes I've taken many times before, in the spirit of friendship and frothy sexual liaison. I walk past the primary school and head down the hill to the high street. On the way, a glass structure, the town college. A monolith of modern design standing in place of the old Johnny Walker edifice. I can feel the world changing around me. A Brion Gysin flicker show.

It was Karl Marx who noticed that Kilmarnock was a haven for transgressive refuseniks. If only his observations had been a little more tactfully articulated. He observed while standing outside Blacks Bar in Dean Street that this particular heterotopia had transcended fiction and become rife with "thieves and criminals of all kinds, living on the crumbs of society, people without a definite trade, vagabonds, *gens sans feu et sans aveu*..... discharged soldiers, discharged jailbirds, escaped galley slaves, swindlers, mountebanks, *lazzaroni*, pickpockets, tricksters, gamblers, *maquereaus*, brothel keepers, porters, literati, organ-grinders, ragpickers, knife grinders, tinkers, beggars....this scum, offal, refuse of all classes." Kilmarnock was a Jean Genet novel. Of course,

Marx is a bit of a prick in this regard – he flaunts an evident moral contempt and political loathing for this complex anthropological group and in his mind the journey from Broken Boy to Transgressive Man is something to be ashamed of. We know that deprivation in modern society cannot be typified by the simple Dean Street degenerates on Marx's lists, neither is this phenomenon exclusive to small-town Ayrshire. In Kilmarnock we are merely products of what the host-body has given us – and of late that hasn't been much. In fact, the state has taken a somewhat morbid ethological approach to its populace: watching our heroin-babies being weaned off the tit and turned on to sausage rolls from behind a pane of reinforced two-way glass. Forget about the Panopticon or other popular social theories of utilitarianism conducive to the betterment of civilised society – let's see what happens when we take everything away and watch the cunts burn. Insidious old Albert Hoffman smudging a fingertip of LSD into his gums. Timothy Leary and Conrad Rooks. Jo Mengele with a more subtle approach. Benway and Schafer breeding giant centipedes. Dr. Moreau taking field notes. The academic gods of Ayrshire are fucking post-punk maniacs. We say to Marx, *get out of Dean Street, ya balmer!*

A group of horny teenagers complain about being bored. Little do they know this is all the work of the malevolent cosmic deities floating above the town, like a vicious wee cunt with a magnifying glass poised over an ant colony – just *waiting* for the sun to come out. Boredom is everyone's affliction. Academics working in the field of boredom concur that boredom results in stimulus seeking. When we observe the switch from behavioural to physiological responses to this state, evidence suggests that boredom increases arousal – which explains all the weans. Research shows that young people tend to seek solace in alcohol and drug abuse, have a greater involvement in extreme sensation activities, and partake in various forms of Burroughsian behaviour. Killie folk often report that there is "fuck all to do" here. Most studies explore the relationship between boredom and alcohol usage among young people in these rural areas, in comparison with young people living in large urban cities. The findings? We're all fucking bored, mate. Marx eventually fucks off to have another affair (and another illegitimate child).

We have always broken our boys here. I'm reminded of the forgotten novelist, Gordon Williams, and his equally forgotten Booker Prize nominee, *From Scenes Like These*. Protagonist: Ayrshire anachronism, Duncan Logan. Logan is fifteen and he's dropped out of school to work on Auld Craig's farm. Logan's life is one of Kafkaesque misery – from the exhausting ritual of daily toil on the farm to his endurance of psychological abuse at the hands of Blackie McCann, Logan's existence presents a brutal relic of forgotten working-class life. The wrong road to manhood; one we have stuck with.

"Can't we move on?" I ask Billy, a regular at Fanny by Gaslight. Billy looks at me with a gleaming vindictiveness. He says nothing, just licks froth from the rim of his pint glass and sighs as if I've spoken about something that no one with any decency would talk about. Something no one has any power over. He curses my effete nature.

"Have a pint," he heaves.

"I'll have a vodka and Coke."

Silence.

Wrong choice.

"Make that a Tennent's..."

The pub bustle resumes. Billy was once a carpet stripper. His whole life. His family worked in the carpet industry and before that they were farmers. His uncle Thomas still has a farm on the outskirts of town. It's what we inherit. A place on the outskirts. It makes that opportunity to expose ourselves in public all the sweeter. It's all we have.

This book wrote itself, but the busted, aching spirit of Scotland's Broken Boys practically willed it.

– Chris Kelso

There are bits and pieces of many cities in Tamaghis. We are walking down a street of worn blue cobblestones rather like the outskirts of Edinburgh when a little boy falls in beside us. About four years old, I think at first. He has a rolling walk like a sailor. He is dressed in shorts with a white sailor shirt and white tennis shoes. I put my hand on his shoulder and he snaps at it with sharp little teeth. "Keep your hands off me, you bastard." And I see that he is a miniature youth of eighteen.

- From *Cities of the Red Night*

Rise of the Ancients

Fear and Loathing, or Pirates and Little Women

Collectivist Ancients in Scotland have dominated and diluted the literary landscape for generations. Even the pirate in Robert Louis Stevenson's *Treasure Island* is a classic model for individualism and its failure – someone who is fearless and takes only for their own gain but who is left with nothing.

With the emergence of the welfare state, a new, more disciplined national identity came to the fore. Lawlessness could be controlled and disciplined by bureaucracy. To emphasise this, Stevenson places Jim Hawkins, an administrative-class civil servant, into the role of hero. The pirates are the antithesis of this order and new national identity of collectivism. However, as Diana Loxley noted, "piracy is justified and justifiable when it provides a vision which satisfies a heroic image of colonial identity." The individual is isolated and vulnerable. The prospering of the collective whole is where contentment lies. To some this is an example of self-control. Ancients want pirates to be more like Little Women. In *Treasure Island*, Jim's ability to adapt is the key to his success. He adjusts to his new surroundings when the pirates appear. He begins to pay close attention to their actions and soon he is imitating aspects of Long John Silver's behaviour. He acts impulsively and bravely when he sneaks onto the pirates' boat in Chapter 12. Jim adapts so much that, by the end of the novel, he shows more courage, charisma, and independence than the captain, squire, and doctor combined. It is the action of a brave individual that maintains order and fosters a sense of community against the threat of institutionalised banality. However, most Ancients will attest that the book reinforces the opinion that it is the collective which is the force worthy of preserving.

In the eyes of the Ancients, Little Women should be married and their rebellion neutralised. They are expected to be subservient to wealthy, successful men. Material richness is something Little Women can only inherit by submitting to prevailing cultural norms, by being good housekeepers and attentive wives. The Moderns know that richness lies at the end of creative freedom and intellectual enlightenment, staples of the true individualist. But self-preservation is the Ancients' only key to accessing happiness.

If ever a country was in need of a rocket up its arse, it was Scotland.

Scotland and the US Cum Together

"The Beast of Birkenshaw"

Pre-Burroughs: In the late fifties the first rocket arrived. Scotland was a nation gripped by fear. There was a killer in our midst and he was smashing the country's post-war fantasy of parochial tranquillity into a thousand easy pieces. On January 1956, Peter Thomas Anthony Manuel followed 17-year-old Anne Kneilands onto an East Kilbride golf course, where he raped her and bludgeoned her to death with an iron bar. This was just Manuel's first execution. Nothing would be the same again. The senseless slaying of Kneilands shocked the country – after all, serial murder, much like taking heroin, is an act of vulgar individualism. In a nation of wanton collectivists, Manuel seemed to represent a seismic shift in ecological perception. Life was imitating art. This was something you'd read about in *True Detective Mysteries* or watch on *Colonel March of Scotland Yard*; it wasn't something you expected to find on your doorstep. Worse still, despite the fact that Peter Manuel was a known sex offender and had been questioned by police, he was released without charge after his father provided him with an alibi. Kneilands' killer walked free. The collective conscious of Scotland could have imploded. *Every man for himself!* they yelled as the mineshaft gave way from above.

Buoyed by his new sense of invincibility, Manuel

then shot Marion Watt, her sister Margaret, and Marion's 16-year-old daughter Vivienne as they slept in their beds in High Burnside, Glasgow. A comically inept police investigation placed Marion's husband at the centre of the murders. Manuel crossed the border, murdering 36-year-old taxi driver, Sydney Dunn, on the 8th of December in Newcastle-on-Tyne. Dunn was shot in the head and had his throat cut. Manuel was in Newcastle looking for work but by the time Dunn's body was discovered on the Northumbria moorland he had already returned home to Scotland. But Manuel wasn't done there. He abducted, raped, and strangled Isabelle Cooke on the 28th of December 1957 at an Uddingston bus stop. Another innocent teenage victim slain. Finally, on the 1st of January 1958, Manuel ended his spree of terror by breaking into the home of the Smart family. He shot Peter and Doris Smart and their ten-year-old son Michael. He stayed in the house for a week after he murdered the family, eating their food and bizarrely keeping their cat alive on tins of "Puss & Boots."

Long before Dennis Nilsen[2] started massacring young men, Scotland was not accustomed to the mindless whims of a deranged serial killer – one who killed whole families, no less. It's not hard to imagine that a boy growing up in the Presbyterian nightmare of Lanarkshire might take leave of his senses among all the boredom and misery, but interestingly this killer was actually born in New York City

2 Denis Nilson was a Scottish murderer and necrophile who killed at least twelve young men between the years of 1978 and 1983.

– that thriving metropolis of drugs, thugs, and queers. Peter Manuel had been baked in the furnace of Hell's Kitchen before he was sent across the Atlantic to Scotland, hot and ready to sting the fingertips of any virtuous native who dared touch him. Newspapers were quick to pick up on his American roots – after all, there was no way a local boy could descend to such depths of depravity, not when he'd been reared on an internationally revered Scottish education system like ours! There must have been some poisoning of the well that hadn't been accounted for. It wasn't long before the media sussed an angle – he was the bastard son of a dangerous one-night dance with the devil. The product of an unholy union. When Scotland and the US came together, sometimes demon spawn like Peter Manuel came shooting out in a puddle of afterbirth. No doubt Scotland had simply been duped into adopting a yank delinquent. Manuel's actions were perhaps the first rumblings of cultural insurrection. The disintegration of our rigid kailyard delusion complete. Tectonic plates were shifting. We were in need of a new "stateless novel." I suppose we have America to thank.

Peter Manuel was hanged at Glasgow's Barlinnie Prison. His last words were "Turn up the radio and I'll go quietly."

Figure 1 Peter Manuel

We may have step-fathered our very own serial killer, but the sixties were dominated by transmissions of American endeavour. Across the country, Scots tuned in with vicarious delight to the latest updates on the costly and contentious Vietnam War. Ayrshire housewives cowered behind plates of stoved potatoes as civil rights protests and the Cuban Missile Crisis brought portents of a bleak future full of apocalyptic social disorder, while the assassinations of US President John F. Kennedy and Dr. Martin Luther King reminded us that good men often die under unjust circumstances. In Scotland? Well, we had moved on from the kailyard and found ourselves stuck in the heart of a folk-rock revival. Our first nuclear power station was built. The Forth Road Bridge opened.

The North Sea oil industry flourished. A quarter million miles away, Americans took man's first steps on alien soil, and Fifers took it too. There was an outbreak of Flower Power and Free Love – and with it, the bellwether drag queens and intellectuals of New York City were collaborating in Andy Warhol's East 47th Street Factory studio with orgiastic abandon. America had gone to the dogs, and we fucking loved it.

Scotland in the sixties remained a largely industrial cityscape of towering iron sentries and twisted metal. Men from the west of Scotland were working hard in mines or on shipyards and the academic elite were attempting to usher in a new age of enlightenment. Elvis Presley famously made his only UK pitstop at Glasgow's Prestwick Airport after doing military service in West Germany. We were happy to have him, for a short while at least. People were mesmerised but highly suspicious. We must have known that Burroughs was coming soon after.

International Writers Conference

"We are imposing no prohibitions on the free expression of opinion, however controversial or unusual" – John Calder

Burroughs, rocket number two, first arrived in Edinburgh in 1962, attending the International Writers Conference. He was living in the capital with Alexander Trocchi and Trocchi's doctor, Andrew Boddy,[3] who provided both men with a profusion of uncut heroin. One day in the city and already their anti-social lifestyle could be described as "the commitment of exile." A pirate and a murderer. Two

3 Boddy appeared briefly in John Calder's 2001 memoir. As well as writing heroin prescriptions for Burroughs and Trocchi, he also offered digs to Wole Soyinka. Boddy went on to be an important figure in the realms of public health research and practice in Scotland, establishing the Social Paediatric and Obstetric Research Unit at Glasgow University.

Broken Boys.

John Calder, however, was an elegant, grouse-shooting sort of fellow who happened to be a closet degenerate. Calder was bullet-bald, hard-faced, and resembled some sort of a medieval judge, but he had a Beat spirit and with the help of Sonia Orwell[4] and Jim Haynes,[5] was responsible for organising the most important conference in Scottish literary history – an event that sought to bridge a gap between the stagnant conservatism of the fifties and the experimentation of the early sixties.

Calder was well-versed in the language of controversy long before his stint as ringleader to the rabid Ancients and belligerent Moderns. Despite being born in Montreal, Calder had established a firm political presence in Scotland, standing for the Liberal Party at two elections against the former prime minister, Sir Alec Douglas-Home, at Kinross and West Perthshire. He believed in freedom for the people and would have died by those principles. But it was as a fearless publisher of underground literature that he will be best remembered. He singlehandedly brought the translated works of Samuel Beckett, Henry Miller, and Leo Tolstoy to Scottish shores and with this new diet of fiction in place it wasn't long before underground journals began popping up throughout the country. Calder also happened

4 Sonia Orwell was the second wife of writer George Orwell.

5 Jim Haynes was a member of the UK underground involved in the founding of Edinburgh's Traverse Theatre and the paper International Times.

to be a mastermind of publicity, orchestrating cultural upheavals across the land by bringing free speech and innovative theatre to the Edinburgh Festival. The national establishment feared him, and with good cause: here was another mongrel seed, this time the product of a squalid tryst with Canada, hell-bent on stirring the pot. It's not an exaggeration to say there had never been anyone quite like him on the national landscape, nor has there been anyone since. Calder, a man so staunchly anti-war and imbued with a self-shaped theistic bhakti that he would make most monastery goers bow their heads in shame, was well-travelled too. He had dined with Burroughs, Beckett, and Barney Rosset[6] at the Grand Séverine the year before and the four men struck up a friendship of mutual admiration. Upon returning to Scotland, Calder used his political sway and silver tongue to convince Lord Harwood to host another event in Edinburgh. It was to be an event that would change everything. His wish was granted. A five-day conference was scheduled for the 20th to the 24th of August. It was here that Burroughs cemented his friendship with Scotland's own junkie-bard, Alexander Trocchi.

Trocchi was widely respected for his work as editor of *Merlin*,[7] although he was considered to be a complex and manipulative disintegratory nihilist – a man who

6 Barney Rosset was the owner of Grove Press and editor-in-chief of the magazine Evergreen Review.

7 Trocchi also gained plaudits as one of the first to actively promote the work of Samuel Beckett and published Eugene Ionesco in English.

8 Lyn Hicks, a 21-year-old American and Trocchi's second wife.

once pimped out his own wife, Lyn,[8] to meet the expenses of his chronic heroin addiction. Nevertheless, he was a talismanic figure in the burgeoning Beat movement of the early sixties and his presence in this story is significant. To Burroughs at least, he was a man worth knowing. Of course, Trocchi and Burroughs could be considered two sides of the same coin. "Cosmonauts of inner space." Both were writers of an unrepentant *avant-garde* fiction. Both had horrible heroin habits. Trocchi and Burroughs would also, down the line, wind up bereaved fathers. But therein, perhaps, the similarity ended. Burroughs was a wraith-like, anti-social junkie who would shoot up in the private seclusion of his hotel room. Trocchi would frequently shoot up in public places (or on live television), grinning and goading passers-by as he went about his practice. Burroughs was a mule of shame. Drugs were his affliction. Trocchi was a dancing monkey hell-bent on dismantling the Scottish parochial fallacy. Drugs were his muse.

It was also here in the capital city that stuffy political clack-box, Hugh MacDiarmid (clad in kilt), famously rose from his throne to dismiss Burroughs as "all heroin and homosexuality." It is entirely possible that Burroughs thought this an underhanded compliment on the part of MacDiarmid. In the 1988 biography, *Literary Outlaw*, Ted Morgan described the event as "one of those 'the -lines -are -drawn -and -which -side -are -you -on' running battles between 'ancients' and 'moderns.'" There was a sense, even at the time, that Calder had organised this event knowing full well that it would end in a face-off.

And that's exactly what happened.

Burroughs, in attendance, represented a new wave of rebellious iconoclasts. People who really didn't give much of a fuck about Robert Burns or his significance to the Scottish literary canon. This was the "modern" and not everyone liked it.

Trocchi was quick to the podium, Roman beak raised high in the air, nostrils flared with energy – he seemed to stab the air with it when he talked, like a furious pigeon pecking for crumbs of controversy. Trocchi then infamously claimed to *his* audience that "a lot of what is interesting in the last twenty years or so of Scottish writing, I myself have written it all."

Writer and Neoist pamphleteer, Stewart Home (a man who describes himself as "a proletarian comedian with Tourette's spewing obscenities"), studied the works of Trocchi and Burroughs simultaneously and noted the out-and-out reluctance of the former to embrace his roots. However, Home also believed that as far as he ran, Alex could never outrace his heritage. It marked him like a tattoo. "Obviously Trocchi was marked by his upbringing in Glasgow and when he was dealing drugs in London those who only knew him as a dealer and had no idea of his cultural cachet called him 'Scotch Alex,' because Scotland was strongly inflected in his speech, albeit rather strangely in later life. He was a Scot to anyone who vaguely knew him." Indeed, Trocchi's relocation from Glasgow to Paris in the early fifties had a tremendous impact on his receptivity to the individualist lifestyle. He kept company with many existential writers during his tenure at *Merlin* and he very much embraced the café-society championed by Henry Miller, Boris Vian, Vladimir Nabokov, Albert Camus, Simone de Beauvoir, and Jean-Paul Sartre. In Gillian Tasker's 2015 thesis, *Cosmonaut of Inner Space: An Existential Enquiry into the Writing of Alexander Trocchi*, the argument is put forth that Trocchi's adherence to existentialism was not "an abstract philosophy but a strategic means to achieve existential freedom from authoritarian systems." Trocchi's shame motivated him to become a man determined to publicly exile himself. At the conference in 1962, he had his platform.

The conference was bristling with energy, and not just because of the gawking young students in attendance. Editor and founder of Aleos books, James Pennington, worked with Burroughs on the 1974 essay collection, *White Subway*. Pennington said "it is surprising how many different writers were there. Calder really set up a fascinating clash of interests. What I think is great is how all the homosexuals stood up for each other against the blundering masculinity of the likes of MacDiarmid. Angus Wilson – a real upright upper-class citizen – was the ringleader, along with his mate Gerard Reve."[9]

The potential for networking and collaboration between vibrant minds seemed boundless. With regards to Burroughs or Trocchi collaborating, both men lived anti-social lifestyles that prevented this from happening. They

9 Gerard Reve was widely regarded as the great post-war Dutch author and was also the first openly gay writer in the country's history.

led wilfully chaotic and transgressive lives. Pennington gives a "very sad account" by Dutch writer and outspoken homosexual, Reve, of a time when he was in Tangier (on the invitation of Burroughs) a year or so after the conference. Upon arrival it transpired that Burroughs was away somewhere and that the recommended hotel had no vacancies. "Reve kicks his heels for a few days but, when Burroughs returns, finds he can't get on with coteries of junkies and young Moroccans filling up the places where he hung out and he goes back to Holland. I say sad because those two together could have produced interesting work."

MacDiarmid would condemn both Trocchi and Burroughs as "vermin who should never have been invited to the conference." The conference atmosphere grew tense and MacDiarmid had no hang-ups about coming across as unwelcoming.[10]

Still, Burroughs sensed the significance of the event and the value of his presence, expressing to fellow *succès de scandale*, Mary McCarthy, that he "could not but feel that it would indeed be the *last* Writers' Conference." In a sense it has never been replicated. McCarthy described the conference in a letter to Hannah Arendt,[11] recalling "people jumping up to confess they were homosexuals or heterosexuals ... an Englishwoman describing her communications with her dead daughter, a Dutch

10 It should be noted that Trocchi and MacDiarmid would go on to be correspondents, and indeed friends, later in life.

11 Hannah Arendt was a German-American philosopher and political theorist.

homosexual, former male nurse, now a Catholic convert, seeking someone to baptise him."

And it was McCarthy who would coin the phrase "stateless novel," which she described as an "action painting" that would signal the end of the national novel. Trocchi was after a similar product, something that transcended national borders and which was written with the hard-edge intensity of the commitment of exile. The stateless novel is littered with broken territories located in an alternative world, somewhere that the exiles can prosper – or at least indulge in their individualist lifestyles and practices unjudged, in peace. Dr. Eva Kowalska, teacher of English and Critical Thinking at the University of the Witwatersrand in South Africa, explored the idea of these "counter-sites": shadow corners within society that Burroughs and other transgressive writers of the time would populate with their fictional denizens. Kowalska consults Michel Foucault's formative 1967 essay, "Of Other Spaces," in her argument. Foucault ponders the notion of temporary social and geographical spaces on the outer rims of mainstream society. Kowalska sees these "counter-sites" as versions, however imperfect, of a utopian ideal in which heterogeneity is valued. "They are by nature non-hegemonic, and in the modern context are often the spaces of subculture or deviance; in literature, they are often the setting if not the subject of transgressive fiction. In the work of the Beat Generation writers, scenes such as nocturnal Times Square, the transient lives of migrant worker communities, port and border cities, or downtown rooming houses, can be understood as heterotopias in terms of their liminality, their difference from conformist society, and the sometimes idealised potential for freedom, expression, and experience they are portrayed as holding."

These heterotopias are "outside of all places, even though it may be possible to indicate their location in reality." This may have been a way for Alexander Trocchi to write about Scotland *outside* of Scotland. A Scotland of his own making. Indeed, further down the line the Modern would truly embrace this idea of statelessness – even writers who were famously patriotic would use this idea of multiple temporalities in a single space. Take Alasdair Gray's[12] ground-breaking novel, *Lanark*, for example – even *this* could be described as a stateless novel. Much like Burroughs did with Tangier, Gray sets his story in a recognisable post-war Dennistoun only to morph his city into a counter-site equivalent – namely, the apocalyptic metropolis of Unthank. We see landmarks like the Glasgow Cathedral and the Necropolis transformed into dystopian edifices loomed over by sword-wielding leviathans. *Lanark* presents its central city as one seized by an individual, turned into something altogether new and free.

Kowalska refers to Tom McCarthy's Trocchi documentary, *A Moveable Void*, and the links to Foucault's idea of the ship at sea as a heterotopia, untethered from

12 Alasdair Gray was a prominent, highly respected Scottish novelist and artist. Lanark is widely considered to be his magnum opus.

the world, yet of it, in "Of Other Spaces":

"Burroughs wrote in a letter to Ginsberg, apropos, I speculate, both his writing and his drug use at the time that 'I am going so far out one day I won't come back at all.' Trocchi wonders in *Cain's Book*, the setting and defining image of which is the scow on the dark sea, 'how far out a man could go without being obliterated.' The project is the same: the immersion of self in heroin and the possibility of writing about it. But how they go about it is very different."

It was a perfect summation of Burroughs and Trocchi and their unerring mission to emancipate human consciousness from all political and cultural control. But the conference itself was fast turning into a mutiny.

Something was in the air that day, something potent and dangerous. Gangs of Broken Boys were roaming the streets of Tollcross, Leith, Pilton, and Broomhouse. The South Side and Gillie teams from Gilmerton had heard about *privileged cunts* gathering around McEwan Hall. Meanwhile, the Leith Team and the Tollcross Rebels – the two biggest mobs (resplendent in bowler hats, ankle-length coats, and rolled-up brollies) – were already battling all the way up Leith Walk right into Waverley Station. Scores of bloodied men could be seen running along Gorgie Road and down the steps of Haymarket. The mobs convened and charged down Princes Street looking for innocent skulls to smash. Edinburgh was in a vice-grip of utter chaos. These gangs were the physical manifestation of the culture war simmering within the university halls. They represented the action painting that would dismantle the rigid structure of reality as we knew it.

The 2,300-capacity McEwan Hall was brimming with university students desperate to see the exotic Americans ruffle a few feathers. And it was on day four of the conference, a day devoted to censorship, that Burroughs really stole the show.

"Opinions on what may or may not be published differ widely. In Great Britain the censorship laws have recently been revised and previously banned books such as 'Lady Chatterley's Lover' can now be published. In America there has been an even greater relaxation of censorship and the same applies to many other countries, but there are still others where the trend is towards more censorship. Moral and political censorship will be discussed and writers will say how much censorship they think is desirable and where existing restrictions should be removed."

– From the original conference programme

Following Mary McCarthy at the podium, Burroughs expanded on the consensus that all censorship is essentially mind control. Nothing ground-breaking, but he believed in this axiom more than anyone. It was determined that the Ancients might espouse "the necessity of protecting children" as a sufficient reason for its implementation, yet the young are "already subjected to a daily barrage of word and image, much of it deliberately calculated to arouse personal desires without satisfying them." Burroughs' philosophy was an open criticism of the traditionalist adherence to the moralism of the Fall, where there was a concerted focus on classification, articulating the opposites, and making judgements on absolutes: black and white, good and evil. Victoria Sackville-West[13] and Rebecca West[14] tutted from their pews as sunken eyes glared at Burroughs on his soapbox. MacDiarmid wriggled in his seat with an indignant expression on his face, one that revealed a man who sensed an imminent dethroning. The old guard were mumbling in the bleachers, forming a mass rebuttal that the ungrateful American interloper wouldn't soon forget. But it was another foreigner, Norman Mailer, whose turn it was to twist the knife, adding that censorship was in keeping with the orthodox values of the Ancients in attendance; that sexual literature like *Naked Lunch* might "weaken warlike potential because it tends to drain it."

13 Victoria Sackville-West was an English novelist, designer, and former lover of Virginia Woolf.
14 Rebecca West was a journalist and travel-writer.

MacDiarmid was visibly furious at the insinuation that he fed on a readership swaddled in impotent victimhood and parochial fantasy. This was becoming more than mere mutiny; it was a castration of sorts. An attempt at inverted censorship. Maybe even, by day four, this was an eye for an eye. Mailer was already an admirer of Trocchi, following the publication of *Cain's Book*. Along with a young Leonard Cohen, Mailer funded Trocchi's emancipation from New York to Montreal[15] where he then boarded a trawler to Aberdeen. MacDiarmid eventually ascended from his throne in outrage before Stephen Spender[16] interjected to veer discussions away from such provocative waters.

Figure 2: Burroughs and Stephen Spender

15 Trocchi was evading an inevitable prison sentence after taking heroin on live television while already on bail.
16 Stephen Spender was an English poet, translator, literary critic, and editor.

Mission accomplished. Of Trocchi, Home considers the Hugh MacDiarmid slur to be rooted in reality – in fact, Trocchi would have taken this insult as a flattering remark: "Oh, he's cosmopolitan, something that includes his being Scottish as we can see so strongly in *Young Adam.*"

Other "cosmopolitan scum" in attendance included Compton MacKenzie, James Baldwin, Henry Miller, Roberto Fernando-Retamar, Angus Wilson, Sonia Brownell (widow of George Orwell), and Margaret Drabble.

Outside of Scotland, the *Transatlantic Review* went on to publish Burroughs' spoken-word pieces from the Edinburgh event, including his four writings devoted to censorship: *Censorship, The Future of the Novel*, *Notes on these Pages*, and *Nova Police Besieged McEwan Hall.* His exploits had become international news.

Prior to the 1962 conference, Burroughs was already a known quantity in Scottish literary circles since, in 1959, an issue of the *Edinburgh University Review* entitled "Jabberwock" published the opening chapter of *Naked Lunch.* "Jabberwock" is a clear reference to Lewis Carroll's nonsensical poem, "Jabberwocky," which centred around the slaying of a mythical beast called the Bandersnatch and featured in his 1871 novel *Through the Looking-Glass, and What Alice Found There.* After a meeting with the White King and White Queen, Alice stumbles across the "semiotic catastrophe" in question. Of course, she soon realises that in this upturned world the verses on the pages must also be etched in some kind of inverted prose that makes perfect sense to the citizens of this land. Upon this realisation, Alice turns a mirror to one of the poems and reads the reflected verse aloud. Part of the original purpose of "Jabberwocky" was to lampoon the pretentious national *literati* of which Carroll himself felt alienated and exiled. A girls' school in Boston requested Carroll's permission to name their school magazine *The Jabberwock* and he was responsive to the idea that the modern youth might derive strength and meaning from a moniker rooted in his work, replying gleefully, "The Anglo-Saxon word 'wocer' or 'wocor' signifies 'offspring' or 'fruit.' Taking 'jabber' in its ordinary acceptation of 'excited and voluble discussion,' this would give the meaning of 'the result of much excited and voluble discussion.'"

It was a bold move to include the "And Start West" section of *Naked Lunch* in a radical but freely available publication, one which was sure to generate discussion among its readership – especially given the story's controversial subject matter.

"And Start West" centres on Burroughs-facsimile, William Lee, who is evading police on a New York subway train. Lee overhears the various drug-babble of the other passengers. While Scotland has always produced its share of self-preserving Ancients, in later years it has also given birth to some outrageous and dangerous artistic minds – and the mere existence of the "Jabberwock" issue of the *Edinburgh Review* shows it wasn't all a bunch of *bildungsroman*. This issue also featured work by Allen

Ginsberg and Gregory Corso and remains an important artefact in the alternative canon.

Edwin Morgan wrote that "the Scottish Renascence has begun to loosen its hold on life [resulting in] a gap between the literary and the public experience which is surprising and indeed shocking in a country as small as Scotland."

The feeling was that this disparity would lead to a New Provincialism, which Morgan didn't want. The Internationalists had executed a successful putsch at the conference, but a country as tiny as Scotland cannot help its incestuous nature. While Morgan would go on to become editor of the dreary *Scottish International* magazine, the national literary scene was so small it meant that all factions, *avant-garde* and insular, were forced to engage with one another on some level. Unsurprisingly, the *avant-garde* and the mainstream would soon coalesce. There were many reasons for this, the limited publishing infrastructure being one. Writers were competing for space in any available medium. "Little magazines" such as *Poor.Old.Tired.Horse*, *Sidewalk*, and *Cleft*,[17] as well as student publications such as *Gambit* and the *Glasgow Review*, featured a mix of Black Mountain poets, European existentialists, and Scottish writers in an attempt to reinforce the more innovative aspects of the literary hegemony.

In 1959, Burroughs contributed to these "little

17 Burroughs contributed "Martin's Folly" to Cleft 1 and "A Distant Hand Lifted" to Cleft 2

magazines" with some regularity. Expat publisher, Alex Neish, was instrumental in bringing Burroughs' work to Scottish shores. Neish argued that Beat writers rescued him from "Scottish prejudice and provincialism." He told *Scotland on Sunday*: "I grew up in Scotland and had led a very parochial life so the Beat poets were a tremendous breath of fresh air. I thought they were really quite outstanding."

Falkirk-based Burroughs expert, Graham Rae, claims "It was Allen Ginsberg who sent Alex Neish 'And Start West,' the classic first chapter of *Naked Lunch*, to use in 'Jabberwock.'"

Neish was a long-standing admirer of Burroughs and published "Have You Seen Slotless City?" from the still in progress *Soft Machine in Sidewalk* #2. Jennie Skerl had this to say about the image of Slotless City: "Slotless City is a futuristic fantasy of violence and pandemonium produced by sexual conflict. Through insoluble conflict the Nova Mob[18] seeks to destroy the earth, and the Slotless City fantasy envisions sexual conflict as the cause of a future apocalypse."

Slotless City declares a state of "total pain, total alert, total war" between men and women. The streets of Cut City, Interzone, are a battlefield of severed limbs and broken glass. Again, we see Burroughs exploring the heterotopias of his own inner space. Burroughs details alternative methods of reproduction that result in a new

18 The Nova Mob were a gang of intergalactic criminals who declared war on the Nova Police.

superhuman organism called "The Property." Of course, the story ends with the destruction of all life on earth.

The apocalypse is communicated in abstruse cut-up imagery. Burroughs recommends that we take our Life Scripts to Cut City and turn it into the Slotless Metropolis. He might be making a subconsciously-articulated point here – that the disintegration of present reality constructs is an effective method of liberation from control. It might be the only instance in Burroughs' life where he achieved this in such a pure way. Amid the strange advertisements for *Scottish Field and Blundell Rulers* and *Sidewalk* #2 is an extraordinary little publication. It contains seven lovely pieces from Edwin Morgan and the quarterly comment, entitled, 'Are you saved, brother, are you saved?' documents the seized copy of Francis Pollini's novel, *Night*, from the home of Alex Neish and Hugh MacDiarmid by Scottish Postal Officials – a comically ridiculous act that only the joyless Scottish authorities could have orchestrated.

Rae believes the little magazines were instrumental in encouraging national change, "even if only as a precursor of the eventual avalanche of American words that would end up transforming the Scottish tongue and artistic and general cultural aesthetic. But in a more general sense, Neish was breaking open – at that time – Scottish parochial provincial writing with the strength and sureness and arrogance of a headstrong young man, and it sounds like that's what it needed in the late fifties, to rid it of hills and heather and haggis and Highlands and shite."

Burroughs biographer, Barry Miles, discussed an early affinity with Scotland: "Before he moved back to New York in 1974, he asked John Calder to look into real estate in Scotland for him, somewhere near Edinburgh, so he obviously liked it there. In the end New York won out because he was offered a teaching job there, but Scotland was his first choice when he decided to move away from London."

But Alex Trocchi was already a staunch anti-Scot in search of the stateless novel and saw his home country as a nation of "stale porridge." He once declared "I hate being Scottish" – a line hijacked by Trocchi exponent, Irvine Welsh, in his post-Beat novel, *Trainspotting*. Despite contrasting feelings about Scotland, Burroughs' rankling of the old guard would've no doubt endeared him further to Trocchi. Burroughs could see the self-hatred of the Scots. He saw through the blinkered patriotism for what it was – the Reichian armour of self-preservation. We were a country steeped in shame. Marinated in it. We had all executed our wives by mistake. We had all indulged and been burned. Fucked and fucked up. We all secretly ached for freedom from behind the iron rods of our own insular jail cell. James Grauerholz corroborated Burroughs' interest in returning to Scotland. "If he talked about living in Scotland, it was undoubtedly to do with Jimmy Page, Aleister Crowley, Kenneth Anger, and an amazing young estate dealer named Perry Press — who sold to Page Crowley's remote castle."

Perry Press was the founder of Pereds[19] and boasted friendships with rock luminaries like the Beatles, Ronnie Wood, Rod Stewart, Eric Clapton, Van Morrison, Pink Floyd, and Led Zeppelin. Press was considered by the rich and influential to be something of a miracle worker. A buyer's agent. Unjudgmental. Press sold Friar Park at Henley-on-Thames to George Harrison, Box Mill near Bath to Peter Gabriel, a stately mansion in Plumpton Place in Sussex to Jimmy Page, and a farm on the Welsh coast to Robert Plant (where Press also managed to secure a flock of 300 sheep for free). His dictum was: "The problem with being a selling agent is that you can't choose to sell only what you like." This bespoke approach to real estate meant he knew how to find a home that suited Burroughs' more insalubrious proclivities. Burroughs liked drugs and attractive young men. Press urged him to consider a number of new-home destinations in the early seventies, including Guatemala and Costa Rica. Scotland was also on this list. This is substantiated in a letter to John Calder in 1973, in which Burroughs requested information on prices and living conditions in Scotland. In his correspondence with his boyfriend and hustler John Brady later that month Burroughs mentioned, "I have been considering the purchase of a remote property in Scotland to carry out my experiments." Burroughs had been investigating sound (specifically with tape recorders) for pseudo-scientific purposes. It seems he had started to conceive

19 Pereds was the first property consultancy specialising in advising and assisting buyers.

of the tape recorder as an augmentation of the human nervous system, one that might work as potential apparatus for paranormal adjustments to reality – and even as the basis for an alternative to psychiatry.

Grauerholz went on, "I think a lot of Press' motivation, and why he brought these things to Burroughs in the latter's late fifties, was a version of 'the seduction of the Mediterranean,' i.e. an idyllic environment of very young men, sexy and beautiful, impoverished, and willing."

Could the slum rats of the Scottish ghettos have appealed to Burroughs' volcanic predilection for vulnerable young Broken Boys? After all, Burroughs had lived only a short walk from London's Piccadilly Circus – an area famed for its boy-hustler marketplace. "Not for nothing, I mean. It was Antony Balch who led him to Duke Street and Dalmeny Court; and 'Tony' was every bit as keen on cottaging as any Orton — or Jarman — or Turing."

Another important figure Burroughs met while in Glasgow was future poet laureate and Scots Makar, Edwin Morgan. Both men had shared a publishing credit in the *Sidewalk* journal but until then had been only distant enthusiasts of each other's work. At the time of their first face-to-face meeting, Morgan was heavily involved in the international concrete poetry movement. Morgan had referred to (and praised) Burroughs in his essay, *The Beat Vigilantes*, written shortly after the 1962 conference. Morgan described William S. Burroughs as the "star performer" of McEwan's Hall – and it seems the young Glaswegian poet was greatly inspired by the verve and creative enthusiasm of his American brethren, even openly taking his countryman, MacDiarmid, to task.

Of Burroughs, Morgan said: "His theme was 'The future of the novel is in space not time'... he doesn't want a story that moves steadily along in time, but an exploration of life in all its dimensions, using techniques like the flashback of cinema, what he calls the cut-up and fold-in methods."

Morgan saw the makings of the irreducible stateless novel and the ingredients Burroughs brought to the kitchen table – these being his culturally ambiguous characters, his splicing and dicing of various patois, and his rejection of traditionalism (order) for the radical (disorder). He was one of several Moderns looking for the new world culture. In 1973's *Gravity's Rainbow*, Thomas Pynchon examined a similar state of statelessness, contrasting the tropics of the south with the Christian north – but he took that idea from Burroughs, who had explored this topic in depth some ten years prior. Morgan waxed lyrical about Burroughs any chance he could. He was so stimulated by Burroughs' work and methodology that he went on to document an account of the Edinburgh Conference in the cut-up style, entitled, *The Fold-In Conference* – which he dedicated to Burroughs. The experimentally-stylised article was first published by the student publication *Gambit: Edinburgh University Review* in Autumn 1962, which was acknowledged by a flattered Burroughs in a letter to Allen Ginsberg: "*Gambit*, the Edinburgh University magazine, has a cut up of the writer's conference in the current issue dedicated to me..."

Following Burroughs' death in August 1997, Morgan accepted an invitation from Rupert Loydell[20] to write a piece in his memory called "My Kind of Angel." Morgan submitted "We Do Our Work And Go," a cut-up poem comprised of the last pages of various books by Burroughs – with Shelley's "Adonais" folded in. The final lineof Morgan's elegy said: "Adios Meester, William like a star."

Despite publicly lambasting him at the conference, MacDiarmid's outburst would prove a pivotal moment in bringing Burroughs into the the literary limelight – even prompting Grove Press to order extra copies of *Naked Lunch* to publish in the US for the first time. These conferences were horribly fusty with the stench of Scotland's self-important cognoscenti, but Burroughs' presence proved a welcome tonic. The Edinburgh summit was a rousing success and is considered a key moment in the transformation of our national literature. In a letter to Paul Bowles,[21] Burroughs commented on the fall-out of his Edinburgh experience, declaring, "Looks like we have burned down Edinburgh."

Early doors, the always precognitive Calder sensed

20 Rupert Loydell is a poet, painter, editor, publisher, and senior lecturer at Falmouth University.

21 Paul Bowles was an American composer, author, and translator who lived most of his life in Tangier.

the impact Burroughs had on that room full of students and scholars and believed it was time to capitalise. The Scottish public might just be ready for something new. He set about convincing Burroughs to compile a series of his most experimental writing to be published and disseminated to bookstores throughout the country. Burroughs was grateful for John Calder, who seemed the antithesis of his unreliable French publisher, Maurice Girodias.[22] *Dead Fingers Talk* was the immediate literary result of the Edinburgh conference and Calder's enthusiasm for Burroughs. As selector and redactor, Calder designed *Dead Fingers Talk* to be a kind of Burroughs Reader – a way of micro-dosing public receptors with the heady taste of his next hard push, *Naked Lunch*.[23] Much like the conference itself, *Dead Fingers Talk* was an experiment of sorts. As a literary amalgam of vignettes and sketches bundled together to form an entirely new (anti-) narrative, the collection is somewhat effective and significant – even if initial reviewers weren't entirely convinced of its merit. Jed Birmingham said, "Needless to say, *Dead Fingers Talk* created a stir. For an astounding 13 weeks, letters both praising and damning the novel appeared in the *Times Literary Supplement*. John Willett got the ball rolling with a negative review of Burroughs' work

22 Girodias was the head of Olympia Press and owed Burroughs a large sum of money for book sales. Girodias did everything he could to avoid speaking with Burroughs and frequently ignored his letters demanding royalties or compensation.

23 The title is actually lifted from the line "only dead fingers talk in Braille" from *Naked Lunch*.

simply titled 'Ugh!' Edith Sitwell, Michael Moorcock, Victor Gollancz, Anthony Burgess, and Eric Mottram all got into the act on both sides of the argument."

Dead Fingers Talk has become a rare commodity among Burroughs collectors, and a highly desirable one. The original cover alludes to the author severing his own finger-joint to impress Jack Anderson, a crush of his at the time. At the time of writing this book, Senior Lecturer in the Department of American Studies at Keele University, Oliver Harris, is preparing a new re-print of *Dead Fingers Talk*. Harris maintains that "what made Burroughs' reputation was publicity arising from the Edinburgh conference, one that might have been located in Scotland but whose horizons were thoroughly international."

Harris goes on to draw further parallels between the conference and the book in question, suggesting they are cultural symbionts:

"Calder's idea of a risky festival, open to chance rather than all under control, suggests why the relation between the conference and the book contract that followed from it was more than a business arrangement. *Dead Fingers Talk* was also an experiment of assembled raw material whose outcome could not be predicted."

A few years later, in 1965, Scots playwright and Trocchi confrère, Tom McGrath, went on to work closely with Burroughs during the International Poetry Incarnation at London's Royal Albert Hall. Barry Graham used the relationship between Trocchi and Tom McGrath in his

1995 novel, *The Book of Man* (based on Trocchi's *Cain's Book*), and while on UK soil Burroughs was never far away from the Glaswegian duo. Graham met McGrath in 1989, when he was the Literary Director at the Lyceum Theatre in Edinburgh, and the two stayed friends until Graham moved to America in 1995. Graham said, "It was Tom who turned me on to Trocchi's work. He told me Trocchi used to say of Burroughs, 'When he writes, he's a genius. When he thinks, he's a crank.' I used that in *The Book of Man*, but it was said of the character Mike Illingworth, who's based on Trocchi. There's no character in the book based on Burroughs, but there is a bit when Illingworth, like Burroughs, cuts up a newspaper and believes he can see the headlines of the future by doing that, which Tom told me Burroughs claimed."

The first time McGrath met Burroughs, Burroughs walked out of the room, mistaking McGrath for the American poet of the same name (and who Burroughs considered a communist). Again, it was Trocchi who introduced them to each other.

Graham goes on to explain that, in *The Book of Man*, the scene where Illingworth comes on to Previn by asking if he's ever had a homosexual experience is verbatim McGrath's story of how Trocchi came onto him. The minor character Tim McGuire is based on McGrath.

"Tom told me a story of how he once invited Burroughs to see a play, and Burroughs answered, 'I've got my own theatre.' Meaning, the inside of his own head."

It is worth mentioning the importance of another

writer during this period in Burroughs' life – Helen Adam. There is really no doubt that he was inspired by the collage work of this Dundonian poet and collagist. Adam was the daughter of a Presbyterian minister and was raised in the north-east of Scotland. The outbreak of war in 1939 took her to America and she became part of the San Francisco Renaissance. "The Flesh of Love" is a fine example of Adam's off-kilter patchwork methodology. A python in a state of cranial kinesis, toad in jaw, rests cradled in the bosom of an elegant-looking debutante. "Where Are The Snows" features a woman on a canoe with several man-sized kittens superimposed over it. Adam was a trans-national Scottish American with a dissident and oppositional attitude towards the nationalist literary establishment. She was proof that the sperm of Scotland and the egg of America could come together in a harmonious and creative way. She inspired Gysin[24] and Burroughs to create literary collages, which resulted in a vast "word horde" that Burroughs would recycle across five distinct works.

We are a country of agriculturalists. We should be conjuring enough plant material to protect our fragile clay, to wrap our organs in the stupendous and cosmogonic philosophy of the *Bhagavad Gita*. Our roots should be in art and magic as well as with the blanched soil, damp and eternal. We were blessed with the tonic of wilderness in our blood.

24 Brion Gysin was an English painter, writer, sound poet, and performance artist. He is best known for his cut-up work with William S. Burroughs.

Rules of the Duel

Graham Masterton was born in Edinburgh and was grandson to the Chief Inspector of Mines for Scotland. Before he became a respected genre writer and self-help guru, Masterton socialised with Burroughs regularly – the two even collaborated on a novel: *Rules of the Duel.*

"I first became aware of William," he said, "when *Naked Lunch* was published in England in 1965 and caused a tremendous stir because of its blatant descriptions of sex and drugs and the *avant-garde* nature of its writing."

Masterton had already discovered Beat culture, consuming the works of key figures like Jack Kerouac, Lawrence Ferlinghetti, and Gregory Corso, and was invigorated by the creative freedom of their writing.

"I had read *Lunch* and I wrote to William and told him how interested I was in the way that he wrote and the complete fearlessness of what he was saying. He was living in Tangier at the time. He wrote back almost immediately and we began a lengthy correspondence. I was writing a lot of poetry at the time and self-publishing it in booklets and I used some of his cut-up techniques for some of the poems and he gave me a very positive response to what I was writing."

In order to take advantage of Dr. Dent's fabled apomorphine treatment, during early efforts to wean himself off heroin, Burroughs came to live in a flat in Duke Street in London's West End. At that time, Masterton had just left a local newspaper in Crawley where he had completed four years of training as a reporter and landed a job as deputy editor of the men's magazine, *Mayfair*.

Figure 3: Masterton, Burroughs, and a Scientology representative

Masterton explained: "I met William in his flat and we started to see each other regularly, discussing writing and films and politics and Scientology and everything else under the sun, and going out for meals in nearby restaurants. I found him extremely amusing and interesting, and I suggested that he start to write a regular feature for *Mayfair*.

"That was how The Burroughs Academy started. I knew that many *Mayfair* readers would find it hard going, but it was quite a prestigious name to have in the magazine. I can't recall how many articles he wrote but I have all the magazines in storage. Yes, we were good friends. It was also a great opportunity to meet some of the most prominent Beat writers such as Allen Ginsberg and Brion Gysin. I never forgave Allen Ginsberg for falling asleep on the floor of William's flat, exhausted with jet lag, and spreading his greasy black curls all over my pale suede Italian shoe. I was a total Mod at the time."

Despite his Scottish connections, Burroughs never accompanied Masterton to the old country. Masterton did drive him to the Scientology Centre at Saint Hill near East Grinstead in Sussex when he was researching the religious doctrine. At the time, Masterton described Burroughs' feelings about Scientology as "extremely suspicious."

The two men went under assumed names – William Lee and Graham Thomas – and the whole visit was filmed and photographed by the late Antony Balch.[25]

25 Anthony Balch was an English film director.

Masterton also met Alexander Trocchi a few times. Trocchi was interested in the writing that Burroughs and Masterton were doing together. Masterton describes Trocchi as "fairly bonkers" – once gifting Burroughs a swordstick. He recalls Burroughs lurching around the Duke Street flat, waving the sword and shouting, "Ho there, you ruffians!" and nearly decapitating Ian Somerville[26] in the process. Burroughs, usually reserved and gentlemanly, exposed a different side of himself around Trocchi. They were cosmically bound. Both had been greatly affected by the loss of loved ones: Trocchi having lost his mother at the age of 16 (which he claims gave him "direction") and Burroughs having executed his wife in an alcohol-induced game of William Tell. Burroughs was similarly motivated to write because of Joan's death, but it was a form of therapy. There is a sense that everything Burroughs ever did was in pursuit of some remedy for his crippling soul-sickness. Perhaps therapy was his true obsession. Burroughs didn't have a fantastic track record when it came to taking the road of least resistance, but there was something about Trocchi that made him wary towards the tail end of their relationship. Like the aforementioned Lanarkshire serial killer, Peter Thomas Anthony Manuel, Trocchi was an abyss in a skin-suit: dangerous, unpredictable. In love with chaos and single-minded in pursuit of his interests. Burroughs at least had room in his life for friends and cats.

26 Ian Sommerville was a computer programmer from England who later became Burroughs' lover and systems adviser.

Around this time, Burroughs also wrote the introduction to a book of Trocchi's poems, *Man at Leisure*, where he describes the Scot as a "metaphysical poet." On the surface it's clear what Burroughs means here – Samuel Johnson[27] defined a metaphysical poet as a writer whose work was distinguished by striking turns of phrase, an emphasis on interrogatives and an inventive use of conceits (often focusing on the spoken rather than lyrical quality of their verse). Metaphysical poets were often confrontational by their very nature. Johnson also felt that this type of poetry was often self-consciously clever, but we know Trocchi was confidently intelligent and his writing style could even be described as *un*pretentious. But this confrontational attitude of the metaphysical was very much an emblematic characteristic of Trocchi, the poet and the man. Eva Kowalska adds that both Burroughs and Trocchi are concerned with writing an ineffable experience, an inexplicable choice, a radically different way of being. Kowalska said: "When Burroughs writes in the introduction to *Man at Leisure* that 'perhaps writers are actually *readers* from hidden books. These books are carefully concealed and surrounded by deadly snares. It is a dangerous expedition to find one of these books and bring back a few words' – this seems to be less about the poetry he's meant to be commenting on, and more about Trocchi's prose, but I think it's applicable to both their work in the fifties/sixties. The point of intersection in the

27 Samuel Johnson was an English moralist and critic.

period encompassing *Junkie* and *Cain's Book* is interesting too. But *Cain's Book* turned out to be Trocchi's strongest and defining work; he did other things but in terms of his creative/literary writing, he didn't really move on from this period. This is well documented by various contemporaries of his in *A Life in Pieces*."[28]

Kowalska notes that both men were on very different trajectories, but overlapped quite meaningfully at this juncture, around these texts:

"I mean the years writing and using and living that went into both of them rather than just the dates of publication. They both use the metaphor of 'far-outness,' both in the subcultural sense but also in a spatial sense of striking out, in life and in writing, beyond the horizon, off the map of what of subjective experience has been charted in words."

Rules of Duel started as a scattering of poems about Masterton's own life. This morphed into a story about the way the two men were feeling about London and the world at the time, socially and politically. It is a brilliant and brightly inventive experiment and worth picking up.

"William invented some of the characters, especially Motherwell the Everlasting Executioner. The reporter character is me...I had just broken up with my girlfriend at the time and was feeling a bit sorry for myself. I would make notes while we talked about the story and then I would go back and type it all up. The next time we met

28 A biography of Trocchi by Allan Campbell and Tim Neil.

we would cut up the sentences to give them a different meaning."

Although the two men struck up a deep friendship, it was always Burroughs' intention to go back to the US. They both went out for dinner with Brion Gysin to a Lebanese restaurant in Covent Garden. It was the time of the Arab-Israeli conflict, and after several glasses of whisky Burroughs started thumping the table and shouting out, "Bomb the A-rabs! Bomb the A-rabs!" Masterton recounts the manager coming over and asking the party politely to leave. Gysin and Masterton supported the drunken Burroughs all the way back to Duke Street, where they dumped him on his bed.

Masterton said: "After that evening I got involved with a girl and he went off to New York and I never saw him again."

DO WHAT RON SAYS
NOW!
GO TO SCOTLAND
GET CLEAR
GO O.T.

The Edinburgh Org

Six years later, in the spring of 1968, Burroughs returned to Auld Reekie, spending a week at the Scottish Scientology Centre on North Bridge at the Hubbard Academy of Personal Independence, aka the "Advanced Org." Burroughs was a religious experimentalist, forever perusing the spiritual marketplace for the latest sacred fix.

Scientology appealed to this sense of curiosity. Something that would finally rid him of the black mark inside, the lingering guilt he felt on a daily basis and which manifested in dreams of supernatural malignance. Something to exorcise Joan Vollmer's floating head, which emerged from the sober darkness whenever he closed his eyes at night. Something to mend the broken boy inside, the one pretending to be a pirate. Burroughs bought into the idea that his spiritual ailments were the result of an inflamed and experience-charged Reactive Mind. In Scientology, this refers to the section of the brain that is unconscious and functions on stimulus-response. Hubbard taught that this was the source of our emotional and psychosomatic disorders. Burroughs drew up correlations between the Reactive Mind and the Mayan calendars, which he believed to be "one of the most precise and hermetic control calendars ever... on this planet, a calendar that in effect controlled what the populace did, thought and felt on any day." He ached for freedom.

L. Ron Hubbard had spread his message far and wide across Europe to emphasise the standard technical application of the religion. Edinburgh would run a Class VIII Auditor Course aboard the flagship, Apollo (previously "The Scotsman") and be attended by top auditors from churches around the world. Hubbard always had his eye on high-profile followers, claiming that "by rehabilitating the artist one does much for rehabilitating the culture." With this motivation, the first Scientology Celebrity Centre was established in 1969.

James Pennington remembers that "Burroughs went up to Edinburgh for I think a few weeks just to finish off his OT clearance. The Scientology crowd are still active up there. And in the very same building too! He only went up there because that was quickest way to become an Operating Thetan and the place had just opened and was keen to get throughput / turnover."

There is much debate about who accompanied

Burroughs to Scotland, but most sources are of the opinion that he must have travelled alone – Scientology's paranoid practices would have kept "students" separated. John Calder is said to have provided Burroughs with temporary housing but Hubbard would not want anyone comparing notes.

In the late sixties, one of the main figures of the Edinburgh scene was Robert Kaufmann, a musician from the US who travelled to Scotland to spread the good word. Kaufman moved about for a year on the fringes of the group but went in pursuit of the prestigious "secret processes." It's possible the two men crossed paths. Both eventually became vocal detractors of Scientology ("suppressives" in cult jargon/Scientologese), and Burroughs praised Kaufmann's exposé, *Inside Scientology,* as a work of "great courage," suggesting the two men may have had some passing association or mutual respect.

But it was in Paris a few years before that Burroughs first learned of Scientology from Brion Gysin and Jacques Stern.[29] Burroughs had fallen out of love with psychiatry and it was time to fill the void with something else. It didn't take long for Scientology to become one of his most intense fixations, matched only by his advocacy of apomorphine (which he believed to be an effective metabolic regulator). After completing the *Nova Trilogy*, Burroughs enrolled at Saint Hill and was audited. He spent the first half of 1968

29 Jacques Stern was a somewhat mysterious figure also known as the "mad baron." He liaised with Burroughs and wrote at the Beat Hotel in Paris, 1959. Burroughs noted that Stern wrote a novel called The Fluke in nine days.

studying Scientology there, becoming a "Clear" (defined as someone who is free from the negative emotions of the Reactive Mind) and converting to "Operating Thetan." The auditing process threw up some intrusive and strange questioning that went along the line of:

"Would you kill small animals in a hunting situation?"

"Do you twitch at night or shake involuntarily during the day?"

"Would you be suspicious of people seeking to borrow money?"

But there was an idea that these questions would help unpick the hardened scab of reality. In a country with multitudinous scabs across its canvas, Scientology has instituted its somewhat sinister, subcutaneous presence – and, on 28 February 2007, the General Register Office approved its first Scientology minister to solemnise Scientology marriage ceremonies in Scotland. It seemed as though Scientology had finally penetrated the mainstream.

Although Scotland does not require any form of official registration for religious groups, it does acknowledge new religions through the registration of ministers to engage in weddings (a minister must be registered as a religious-marriage celebrant). This registration process is regulated by Section 9 of the Marriage (Scotland) Act 1977, meaning a religious party (out-with the Church of Scotland) may nominate its members to the Registrar General for solemnisation. The Association for Better Living and Education, a minor branch of Scientology, put up sponsored stalls at Labour and Conservative Party conferences in 2006. The name was sneaky and misleading; the group really just wanted to promote Narconon, their drug rehabilitation programme, advising children to avoid addiction by taking saunas and eating cod liver oil tablets. Since then, the Church has failed in bids to occupy the Lothian Chambers and establish a secret golf club called "Scottish Highland Quietude Club." Its presence is menacing and it's been that way since the sixties.

Just like his cut-up technique, Burroughs believed that Scientology could be an evangelical tool of freedom from social control and diluted consciousness, and so it was worth the 80 hours of auditing at the Advanced Org to become Clear (number 1163). The Edinburgh course cost Burroughs £1,500 before he was eventually accused of "treason" in April 1969 for his public criticisms of the Sea Org and he left soon thereafter. He never did completely rid his body of those pesky Thetans though.

The Edinburgh Org is not without its own distinctly dark roots. There were strange deaths and underhanded practices even in the sixties. Around the time Burroughs started his course, James Stewart, a thirty-five-year-old encyclopaedia salesman, was suspended from the Edinburgh Org because he had a "history of epilepsy and as such was refused permission to continue Scientology training." Stewart's name was spotlighted as a "condition of doubt" on account of his having seizures in public. He had recently suffered a fit and injured his head, which – in the eyes of the Church – called into question the validity of Scientology.

In *Inside Scientology*, Robert Kaufman explained that Stewart was made to do chores for 80 hours straight as punishment for his seizures, which they called an "Ethics Condition." However, while performing his penance, Stewart wore a blood-stained bandage. The Org were appalled and determined to rectify this afront by having him crawl across the perilously steep slates of the building's roof during the final stage of a Doubt Formula.[30]

The *Observer* reported that Stewart had been found dead fifty feet below the open bay window of a hotel, but that it was not a suicide.[31] They quoted his wife, Thelma, who was also a Scientologist, as saying she did not know how her husband's death occurred, "but she did know that it had nothing to do with Scientology."

A few days later, Stewart's funeral and cremation notice were posted on a bulletin board in the Edinburgh Org office and Thelma was promoted another level in the organisation. Kaufman initially believed that the 80-hour penalty had contributed to Stewart's death; however, one of Kaufman's Scientology instructors told him that he had heard that James Stewart hadn't really died at all and that it had all been a miscommunication.

30 The Doubt Formula is officially defined as: "Informing oneself honestly of the actual intentions and activities of that group, project, or organization, without listening to unfair opinions or rumours."

31 The public press in Scotland did not print names in suicide cases, but rather incorporated them into the statistics of the annals of the Chief Constables.

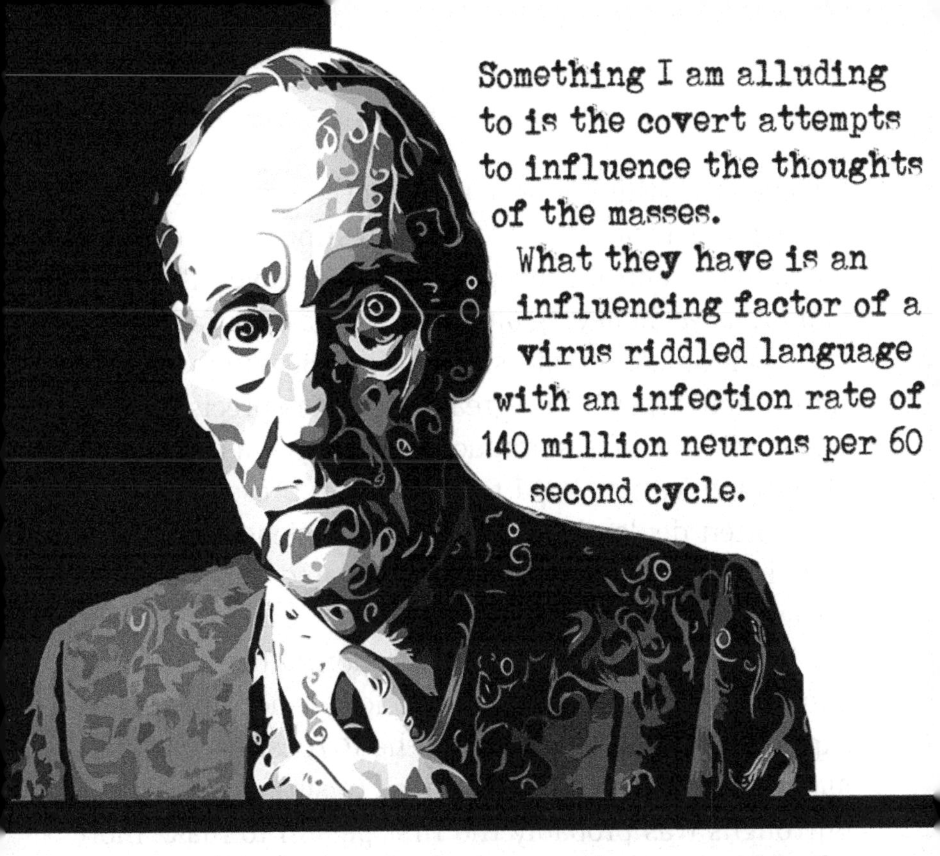

Burroughs had noticed strange goings-on within the Org, noting that all around the Edinburgh office, Xenu's Galactic Confederacy was represented by 26 wreaths.[32] Advanced Org members were encouraged to consult the *Scientologist Technical Dictionary* for appropriate garb, with staff instructed to wear pristine white uniforms with silver boots to mimic Xenu's Galactic Control. In spite of this lunacy, demand for advanced levels continued to increase and the Edinburgh Advanced Organisation was forced to move to larger quarters.

Undoubtedly, incidents like the death of James Stewart left Burroughs unsettled and eager to return to London.

32 Wreaths represent the 26 stars of Xenu's Galactic Confederacy.

But even with this going on in the peripheries, the Church *did* explore ideas that were interesting to Burroughs, including a central concept in his 1962 novel, *The Ticket that Exploded*. Believing language to be a virus, a medium for communication *and* subjugation, Burroughs said of the Church, "they have a great deal of very precise data on words and the effects produced by words – a real science of communication. But I feel that their presentation has been often deplorable and that as a science, a body of knowledge, it is definitely being vitiated by a dogmatic policy."

Burroughs went looking for freedom but instead found another control system. Disillusioned, he documented his experiences with the church in the 1971 essay collection, *Ali's Smile*, which prompted Brion Gysin to remark that Burroughs was probably the first person to make more money *from* Scientology than it got to make from him.

Burroughs then continued to poke fun at the Org and its Orwellian security protocols in *Bill and Tony*, a 1971 short film collaboration between Burroughs and Balch. Here, he recited instructions for how to conduct an auditing session.

He revealed: "They tried to put me into a condition, and I said: 'well, I'm not going to put up with this. Gold stars and all this stuff I left back in Kindergarten.'"

Scientology was far from Burroughs' only crank obsession. Well before he had heard of L .Ron Hubbard, Burroughs was an adherent of Wilhelm Reich,[33] creator

33 Wilhelm Reich was a controversial psychoanalyst known for unorthodox sex and energy theories.

of the Orgone Accumulator, a glorified wooden box said to hone one's creative and sexual energies. Burroughs believed the properties of Orgone could cure cancer and, in 1974, he told David Bowie in *Rolling Stone* magazine that he planned on setting up an institute of advanced studies to explore the Reich's pseudoscientific quackery. He planned on opening the centre somewhere in Scotland.

"Its aim will be to extend awareness and alter consciousness in the direction of greater range, flexibility and effectiveness at a time when traditional disciplines have failed to come up with viable solutions. You see, the advent of the space age and the possibility of exploring galaxies and contacting alien life forms poses an urgent necessity for radically new solutions. We will be considering only non-chemical methods with the emphasis placed on combination, synthesis, interaction and rotation of methods now being used in the East and West, together with methods that are not at present being used to extend awareness or increase human potentials."

This project never came into fruition and we are left wondering what the potential for more national enlightenment could have been.

Ewan Morrison & the Counterculture

Present Day/Kelvingrove Park:
I see a man in the distance, running. I'm meeting Ewan Morrison and the running man fits his description. He leans into the harsh Glaswegian wind, snow bearding the boundary of his face. He collapses against a tree for a moment, then starts running again. He jumps a vacant lot of frozen corn shucks. A common frog mirrors him, soaring into a corpse-lined divet. Weeds and bushes emerge from the undergrowth. Morrison is clearly running from something. From someone.

The reasons for his outlaw lifestyle are clear. Ewan Morrison was part of the burgeoning grunge counterculture in the nineties and his reputation as one of the boy-heroes of Plague City precedes him. Within the Gen-X culture of nihilism, postmodernism, and counterculture was a grounded adoration of characters like William S. Burroughs. Something he has been unable to outrun. We find a quiet spot beneath high clouds laced with silicate particles.

Audio recordings of William S. Burroughs had given his work a revival among Scottish students in the eighties and, according to Morrison, these tapes were like gold dust. They would go on to become part of the youth subculture sweeping the country, perhaps best epitomised in Gus Van Sant's *Drugstore Cowboy*, Irvine Welsh's *Trainspotting*, and the arrival of industrial music that made use of the cut-up technique. Morrison wonders, "Did Irvine read *Junkie*? I wonder who did in Scotland." Even if he didn't, Burroughs' spirit had permeated the cultural consciousness of the nineties.

Morrison looks at me as a swarm of fungus gnats appear in his palm and bury their way beneath the strata of loam and flesh. Time is running out. He cites *Spare Ass Annie,* a collaboration between Burroughs and The Disposable Heroes of Hiphoprisy,[34] as a staple text of the Neo Beat audio era. Gateway drugs to the life of an outlaw. Most people Morrison hung out with after art school in

34 The Disposable Heroes of Hiphoprisy were an American hip-hop ensemble inspired by the Beat generation.

Glasgow had Burroughs' audio and would listen to him sermonise in their Garnethill dorms.

Morrison said: "We used to refer to Burroughs as 'Uncle Bill.' William S. Burroughs' samples from the audio recordings he'd made from the seventies and the nineties kept popping up on albums. His slow droning voice laced with a casual malevolence was the height of nihilistic hip-dom at the time. He showed up on albums like *Smack my Crack* along with the Butthole Surfers, Tom Waits, and Nick Cave. And the album *Spare Ass Annie*, by the Disposable Heroes, was based entirely on Bill Burroughs' audio recordings. He was also in the films we adored – playing [a character] very much like himself in Gus Van Sant's *Drugstore Cowboy*. In 1991 and 1993, we had *The Junky's Christmas* and *Thanksgiving Prayer*. In 1991, Cronenberg struggled to make a film out of *Naked Lunch*; most of us hated it but loved the fact that it existed anyway. And Gus Van Sant and Burroughs released *The Elvis of Letters* – four tracks that were endlessly played in all the underground indie joints that I used to haunt. Great tracks included *The Hipster Be-Bop Junkie* and *Million of Images*. For our countercultural sect in Glasgow, and in many locations around the world, Burroughs was the go-to guru. Grumpy scary old Uncle Bill. We thought he was subversive and we thought being subversive was something to aspire to even though most of us weren't sure exactly what we were subverting. We were in our twenties and this is pretty common for folks of that age – more common still among kids who're caught without anything much to believe in. We didn't realise that nihilism, Burroughs' words, 'isn't worth shit,' and that you end up subverting the ground you're standing on, but that's a different story and one that begins in the 2000s."

Morrison believes it's virtually impossible for people of the millennial generation to grasp the culture of Generation X in the nineties and the role a Refusenik like Burroughs had within it.

"The counterculture I was part of back then, just after art school, was so negative it terrifies both millennials and the baby boomers alike. There was slackerdom, art-rock, indie, queercore, hardcore, industrial music, the fetishisation of S&M, the valorisation of murderers and terrorists as being hip. It was bleak stuff."

For Morrison, Burroughs reflected something of the Scottish youth – disengaged, aimless, and without respect for the safe attitudes of teen idols gone by.

"There was definitely a fetishisation of the psychologically disturbed, a glamorisation of addiction. The baby boomers had Bob Dylan and Joan Baez. We, coming after the punks, took a sadistic and malevolent pride in parading our adoration of figures like Charles Manson (the anti-hippie), Andreas Baader (the terrorist), and Uncle Bill Burroughs had pride of place among our legends. We didn't like Burroughs for his literary style or artistic merit as much as we adored him for breaking all rules of taste."

But why was Gen X slacker culture so nihilistic and lost? Morrison explains:

"It's a good question. Only a few sociologists have tried to fathom this. We occurred just as the Berlin Wall fell and the second great boom of consumerism took hold. A lot of us had been raised with a sense of desperation around what the hell was left of the left-wing project and fed the idea that we had to despise and destroy Western Capitalist Patriarchal culture. For many of us this turned into defeatism and self-loathing rather than any kind of action. You can see this in Kurt Cobain, who collaborated with Burroughs on "The 'Priest' They Called Him" around 1992. The slacker attitude was drop out, fuck the world, take drugs, hate everyone, and being so anti-everything you could almost just about cobble together a sense of self."

Morrison relays that pretty much everyone who was trying to live like this in the Scottish art scenes of the nineties saw Burroughs as a kind of God, a Milarepa. He was the mad junkie who outlived death, enduring this realm as a kind of ghost, surviving on a seething hatred of everything. Burroughs had a playful nihilism. The antithesis of Allen Ginsberg. Burroughs was dangerous. He could mess you up.

"So with my own artistic project, [I started out] hugely immersed in that culture and attitude, absorbing the audio recordings of Burroughs. I found a rare audio recording of the *Nova Convention*[35] (1978) in an anarchist

35 The Nova Convention was a three-day multimedia event in New York City and paid homage to William S. Burroughs. The event featured the likes of Patti Smith, Allen Ginsberg, and Frank Zappa.

bookshop in Camden and it was much prized among my peers. It had sections read from *Naked Lunch* and separate short essay fragments that Burroughs read out on being an explorer of inner space and the necessity of exploring outer space. The question Burroughs asks, and it was also posed by Gysin, is – is there a way out of the oppressive constraints of rational western culture? Burroughs' writing was a series of attempts to escape reason through transgression, addiction, and aesthetic violence."

Morrison missed out on the Edinburgh talk, but the *Nova Convention* became his substitute.

Figure 4: courtesy of James Grauerholz

"It was clear to me that Burroughs, although he came

from beatnik hippie culture, was the one survivor from that mess. He was the negative man, like I say, the anti-hippie. I could identify with this attitude. I'd grown up with hippie parents and I saw the entire hippie project for the bag of magical thinking and lies that it really was. Burroughs was a way out of that, for me anyway. His writing was vile, evil, obsessive. In short: fucked up. There was nothing redemptive about it. I used to get migraines and nausea from trying to read books like *Wild Boys*, and I considered this to be an induction or rite of passage."

Morrison wrote three novels (*Swung*, *Distance*, *Ménage*) that were about characters who were trying to cope with the nihilistic mindset of his generation. Morrison says:

"My characters were looking for an escape through transgression, looking for that way out – like Burroughs said: 'finding God in the flashbulb of orgasm.' To find a way out of this oppressive rational culture by pushing excess to its limit and hoping something would snap, hoping some door would open. That was very much the Burroughs problem, the Gus Van Sant problem, the Cobain problem – they were asking the question 'could you find a way out of a world with no values, by steeping yourself in transgression?' For Cobain the answer was suicide, for Van Sant there was the refuge of the aesthetic, for Burroughs the answer was to live like a ghost endlessly replaying your own escape attempts.

"Of course, Burroughs' cut-up technique was a literary dead end, as was the pursuit of freedom through excess and transgression, but in terms of writing style, I got something important from him, for sure: I realised that it is important to write without being too consciously aware of what you're doing, then to set it aside, cut it up, then re-assemble the text (or throw it away). Cutting together fragments – something Bowie took from Burroughs – is something I also did with *Tales from the Mall* short story sections, but also in the form of the book itself. It's a deliberate contradictory mess of forms – fiction, non-fiction, recorded anecdote, factoid."

In later writing, Morrison tackled the problem of the hippies head-on.

"*Close Your Eyes* is really about a child of the hippies who was messed up by the hippie project (as so many were) and by poor, failed attempts at alternatives to parenting that were the kind of things that radical hippie parents attempted. In *Close Your Eyes*, I wanted the protagonist Rowan to have a hippie childhood but also to be an anti-hippie, so I used Burroughs' cut-up technique to shatter the continuity of her inner voice. There are moments when sections of parenting manuals and hippie songs clash in Rowan's mind, and on the page that took the form of me cutting and pasting un-altered chunks of text from these other texts into her stream of consciousness. It's jarring, abrupt."

Morrison went on: "Most of all, I got from Burroughs the idea that it is important to innovate with the form of fiction itself in order to communicate between the lines, to discover, through experiment, meanings that can't be communicated in straight A-to-B-to-C narration. I think writers like Ali Smith also use this kind of approach. The rational mind, or mine anyway, has to be tricked into communicating things it doesn't realise it already knows. This can be done in many ways. Whereas people like Gysin and Leary would have used hallucinogens, Burroughs heroin, the Romantic poets laudanum, a similar kind of irrationalism can be created through uninterrupted stream of consciousness. Like Virginia Woolf spurting out all kinds of un-reason, then treating the splurge of text later as found footage, to be cut up.

"The central idea in Burroughs needed some refinement. [For me] it was about using the form of text as if it was all found text. Rather than crafting a perfect page, you splurge out ten, then cut them up and re-assemble.

"On other fronts, I think that the resurgence of Burroughs in the nineties was really my generation looking for a voice, something that might offer a way out of the failure of the hippie dream and the failure of the radical left. I tried to tackle that set of problems head on in *Nina X*, [which featured] the idea of a person who was shaped by radical politics of the sixties but who has a fractured subjectivity because of it.

"At the end of the day, Burroughs went as far as he could, but his project was a dead end. An epic and intense failure perhaps. He was the alternative to the hippie project – the ghost-man who took it into darkness and pushed it as far as it could go in search of a gateway, to move from the transgressive to the transcendent. I think of that line from Emil Cioran – 'a book is a suicide postponed' – and I suspect that Burroughs' entire oeuvre was a suicide postponed eighteen times."

Morrison looks up and becomes panicked. He sets off in a northerly direction, across the graphite valleys and recessed wens to the urban ashrams. Neither Morrison nor I can deny these chains. The night weeps its jewels. My body ages another ten years.

There is no denying Burroughs' impact on Scottish counterculture in the late seventies, eighties, and even nineties, but his influence stretches beyond the underground. Jimme O'Neil, lead singer of Scottish stadium-fillers, *The Silencers,* has frequently mentioned the impact Burroughs had on his own writing, but confessed that the comic nihilistic grandeur of *Naked Lunch* was initially lost on him:

"I had a great pal from Garrowhill who I was at school with – Stephen Lang. He was the first singer of my band *Fingerprintz* and we talked about Burroughs a lot. I was a big Kerouac fan and had nearly all his books and so knew about Burroughs from that source. I had also attempted to read *Naked Lunch* as Kerouac praised him as a genius. It was depressing stuff and I think I was looking for something safer at the time. It was with Step (band member Stephen Greer) who was very funny, also gay, that I realised after rereading *Naked Lunch* again that in fact the book was a hilarious surrealistic satire. I then went on to read others."

Step was based at the Coleraine campus of Ulster

University and had friends in Northern Ireland. O'Neil and Step would spend a mad summer together in Port Stewart in 1971 and would almost make a direct connection with their hero, Bill Burroughs.

"I think we spent the whole summer reading books, listening to the furthest-out music, drugs, etc. One of his friends we lived with was a 'poet' guy called John 'Hoppy' Hopkins,[36] who was a Burroughs fanatic. He had ambitions to be a writer. Later Hoppy came to London where we were all living together in Wandsworth. He tracked Burroughs down and would go to see him for a period of about six months. He said, 'Well, if Shakespeare was still alive you would want to speak to him.' I think it would be '72 or '73. He would tell stories about Burroughs and Ginsberg talking together. I can remember asking 'What were they talking about?' He said mostly American politics. I never met Burroughs or Ginsberg. Hoppy was a kind of super fan who was tolerated because he would sit and listen without saying anything. To know about Burroughs though, you really have to call Dr. Benway. Ask for an appointment and he'll give you directions. I never had the balls to do it myself."

36 John 'Hoppy' Hopkins was a prominent counterculture figure in London during the sixties.

Burroughs & Science Fiction

(in conversation with Hal Duncan, Graham Rae, and Preston Grassmann at the Interzone Pub, Glasgow)

I pick up the receiver, place it to my ear, and hear a breathless hunger emerge in distorted surges of barbed static. I can almost picture him on the other line, standing erect, like a parody of the stale, smelly bureaucrat. All awkward angles and perma-tan. The opposite of my aged, sagging body. Dr. Benway.

"I need to make an appointment," I say. Benway snorts. I can make out the contracted muscles of a shit-eating grin as he mocks me. Can virtually smell the expensive cinched suit of untanned sealskin. I keep him on the line, tense my fist around the earpiece until the plastic makes a crack. There is a moment's silence before his hideous belly-laugh blasts down the receiver. I watch the falcate moonlets of Glasgow descend and blush, turning the sky a hue of bloody red that's surely befitting of my inevitable fate at the hands of Benway. The good doctor gives one last condescending cackle, then says "Go to the Interzone Pub," before disconnecting the call. I return to my work – this book – flustered and distracted. A new thirst seizes me, ploughing deep furrows into my throat, and the vulnerability of my humanity makes me balk. The Christ-Eye orbits so close to land that the exoplanet becomes tidally locked, temporarily.

I realise I really need a damn drink.

Across the alien wasteland, morphine tartrate syrettes line the gutters. This is now the land of dips, paperhangers, and pimps. I see the Interzone Pub down Renfield Lane. In the pub window, a familiar face.

"The doctor said you'd come..."

It was at the John Smith's bookshop in Glasgow University back in 1989 when Hal Duncan first stumbled upon the work of William S. Burroughs. Duncan had gone in to buy course texts and was immediately sucked into browsing the counterculture materials at his disposal.

"I remember clocking his books *Queer* and *Junkie*. I think I was still too deep in the closet to browse the first, and the second looked like straight miserabilist realism, but then there was *Naked Lunch* in the current Paladin edition, all white spines and classy-as-fuck looking. I picked up a whack of those Picador titles because it was just a great line of modern classics, so that might have been part of what caught my eye, though it could've just as easily been Burroughs that was the first to hook me; I can't remember now."

The back-cover copy sounded wild and edgy, with a blurb by Ballard casting Burroughs as successor to James Joyce, references to "the Lobotomy Kid" and "his giant centipede."

"I must have noseyed the actual text too, of course. And it all sounded like some amazing drug-fuelled rampage of a novel, like Hunter S. Thompson does Delany's *Dhalgren* or something. I remember being blown away after reading it, when I came to the appendix with a series of letters about the controversy of its first publication, realising how long ago it had been written and what age Burroughs was when he did it. That gobsmacked me, that it could feel so vital, so fresh, decades down the line."

Duncan spent a few years after as a computer programmer but the enduring presence of *Naked Lunch* stayed with the young Ayrshireman, festering and pollinising. In 2005, his Burroughsian speculative fiction novel, *Velum*, was picked up by Pan MacMillan and he set off on a path to writerly success.

"There were too many things I dug about it to list them all, really. I was big into science-fiction and fantasy as a reader and aspiring writer."

Duncan had just joined the Glasgow Science Fiction Writers' Circle and his tastes veered very much toward the New Wave – Delany, Ellison, Moorcock, Norman Spinrad, and Philip José Farmer to name a few. Burroughs incorporated elements of science fiction into his work and it was massively exciting to find this wild card coming at the tropes from outside the genre label.

Like all great speculative fiction writers, Burroughs was a skilled precog, having foreseen AIDS, genetic engineering, liposuction, computer viruses, and the crack epidemic. Without Burroughs the SF genre would never have cyberpunk. Both William Gibson and John Shirley cited Burroughs as major influence. UK science fiction writer, John Brunner (who passed away while at a convention in Glasgow), used many of Burroughs' techniques in *Stand on Zanzibar*. Preston Grassmann said of Brunner's Hugo Award-winning *Stand on Zanzibar*: "the fragmentary text and multiple perspectives are used in entirely new ways. Would that have been possible if it wasn't for work like *Naked Lunch*, *The Soft Machine*, and *The Ticket That Exploded*?"

Duncan went on: "Burroughs was saying 'to fuck with the plot-driven adventure/thriller story formulae.' The non-linearity, the collaging of riffs, the full-on cut-up-and-fold-in chaos where narrative coherence just completely breaks down – that was what I was looking for in fiction. I look at the 'S' in 'SF' as standing for 'strange' – strangeness as the key feature of SF or fantasy or slipstream fellow travellers, strangeness running the full gamut from the marvellous to the monstrous, including the uncanny and the absurd. Where commercial science-fiction and fantasy doesn't like to be *too* strange, can be conservative in just using tropes with a shallow marvellous/monstrous allure, nothing that might actually, Cock forbid, unsettle the reader by being *truly* outré, Burroughs pulled out all the stops."

Burroughs wasn't just ignoring the conventions of aliens and robots in favour of Mugwumps and giant centipedes; he was splitting the very fabric of narrative storytelling.[37]

One need only look at the New Wavers to see Burroughs' influence. Duncan refers to Alfred Bester's typographic trickery in *The Stars My Destination* and *The Demolished Man* as prime examples of an SF icon who stole from the book of Burroughs. But Duncan also appreciated the inherent sexuality of the man's work.

"It was queer as fuck, aggressively so, not gay as in happy, but queer as in 'fuck you.' So it spoke to me like Derek Jarman's stuff, like Delany's. As a child of the seventies, I grew up with images of queerness that were stereotypical effeminacy – Larry Grayson, John Inman, John Hurt playing Quentin Crisp. In the eighties, it was all

37 See Dhalgren with its journal sections interwoven with the main narrative.

Boy George and Erasure and the Pet Shop Boys, and where the fuck, I wanted to know, was the homosexuality that *didn't* play to a camp cliché or fit some template carved out in the gay discos. Part of it was no doubt internalised homophobia, toxic masculinity, but part of it was just... I saw a homonormativity then that you can kinda see now in white gay male culture, in the commercialised bollocks of Pride. I identified with Jarman's Caravaggio, with Rimbaud, with Iggy Pop at his queerest, stripped to the waist, glitter-spangled, but screaming out the 'Looooooooord!' at the start of 'TV Eye.' I'd missed out on punk and felt zero connection to the gay club scene. Burroughs was *my* kind of queer, writing our sexuality as more 'manly' than yer straight male could come close to – more aggressive, more in-yer-face, more take-no-prisoners."

Needless to say, Burroughs had a huge influence on Duncan. He was inspired to write experimental vignettes in a personal iconography that was basically impenetrable to anyone else.

"It was like a noir narrative voice down to those crime style namings like the Lobotomy Kid or whatnot. Burroughs is chockful of characteristic features that are easy to copy, to pastiche. And there's that common thing, when you're still finding your feet, of just emulating shit you think is cool without really having a good reason for it, without it being authentic. So I kinda had to grow out of that, assimilate his influence to a point where it's no longer blindingly obvious because it's not just adoring mimicry."

Duncan suggests that he is philosophically more aligned with a post-transgressive stance: "Like Burroughs revels in the abject and the monstrous, and there's no small vein of misanthropy running through his work. I mean, the very point of that 'naked lunch' image is that the reality of what's on the end of the fork is disgusting when seen clearly, stripped of illusion. Where that chimes with other transgressive works – Delany's *Hogg*, *Salo*, *Last Exit to Brooklyn*, take yer pick – we're past the time of 'Howl' being prosecuted for obscenity, at a point where you can keep breaking taboos to push people's buttons, but if you're just re-treading the ground broken half a century ago, that's not really taking up the torch. There's a risk of an 'alternative' but ultimately commercial (sub)genre approach to the Burroughsian just becoming a mechanism of recuperation, the establishment co-opting the radical, commodifying the pastiche of it as a facile stylish posture of edgelordy. Like, if you're slapping '-punk' on the end of some noun as a label for your subgenre situated wholly in the discourse of science-fiction and fantasy as a marketing category, that's not fucking punk. Sorry. If you're not a fuckin heroin addict being buttfucked by rent boys, pastiching Burroughs's punk-ass attitude just feels like... well, do you really *believe* that?"

Duncan's sympathises less with the profane and perverse taboo-breaking of fiction, identifying its own substance as transgressive and more with what Delany does in *Through the Valley of the Nest of Spiders*.

"It's a frickin' *pastoral idyll* of hardcore fetishistic gay pornography and the sweetest love story you'll ever read. The way it rejects the very concept of 'transgression,' that feels far more where the cutting edge is now than where it was when Burroughs was writing *Naked Lunch.* As it should. We're not in the beatnik era anymore. When you look at my fiction these days then, I think the impact of Burroughs might not be immediately obvious. It's Delany and Davenport I nod to in the homoerotic strangeness of *Susurrus on Mars.*"

Still, there are certainly a couple of deliberate tributes to Burroughs scattered through Duncan's work, like the use of Interzone for the letter "I" in his seminal *A to Z of the Fantastic City* as well as references dropped into *Broken Hearts in Bullet Time* – a Jack Flash story set in the interstices of the movie *Casablanca.* One could easily view most of the Jack Flash stuff in *Vellum* and *Ink* as heavily Burroughsian. There's plenty of fragmentation, even in the nom de guerre monikers of the characters.

"I've no doubt there's an influence in terms of narrative voice too. Along with Delany and Davenport and Joyce, Burroughs is right up there at the top of the list of writers who opened my eyes to prosody, to the cadences of prose dynamics. And here and there you'll find touches of the dark and twisted cynicism, of the grotesque and the Grand Guignol. There's more than a touch of Interzone in my recurrent conceit of New Sodom, a city stitched together from all the gay villages and cruising zones of every city in the world – and in the nightmarish counterpoint to it of Moloch (as per Ginsberg)."

Where *Ink* riffs on the seven souls of ancient Egyptian religious beliefs, it was Burroughs' *The Western Lands* that planted that germ way back when. And Duncan admits that perceptive readers might also pick out and trace back to the source gentle homages that he has forgotten or quirks of writing unconsciously picked up from Burroughs.

As much as Duncan says his sympathies now lie with the post-transgressive, he does think it's telling that in 1989/1990, he thought Burroughs was a contemporary writer.

"I dare say that any unwitting teenager picking him up now might still make that mistake. His work still feels vital, visceral. And it's still going to blow your fucking mind if you've never read anything that wild. With fascism fucking everywhere at the moment, there's no guarantee that all the demolition of what qualifies as obscene won't be rolled back in a resurgence of the reactionary, making something like *Naked Lunch* every bit as revolutionary in the next decade as it was in the sixties; every bit as incendiary. He's a fucking literary Molotov cocktail, and there will always be a place for that, whether it's something you need as a teenager or twentysomething to blow your mind open, expand your horizons, or whether it's something needed in a pitched struggle against the authoritarian cuntfuckery of a society clamping the fuck down. I see no shortage of reasons to read Burroughs for a universal audience right now. And I think he'll always speak to the upstarts among us. That visceral vitality will always be new."

But Duncan doesn't believe there is some sort of national character to the Scottish people giving us a particular affinity with his experimentalism.

"We're having a distinct cultural moment right now, I suppose, with Brexit and the rise of English ethnonationalism galvanising the movement toward independence. There's an inherited cultural cringe born of being a colonial subject (and soldiers of the Empire, of course) for centuries – think Renton's "Scotland's shit" rant in *Trainspotting* – which is turning to an increasingly entrenched defiance. Put in the context of global fascism, we could end up being one of the last wee bastions of a progressive culture abjected as decadence by the reactionaries, a bit of a heaven in a world going to hell. We could maybe imagine something of an underdog mindset, a cynical edge in Scottish comedy from Billy Connolly through to Frankie Boyle, an irreverence in things like *Trainspotting*, literary radicalism in writers like Alasdair Gray."

He is wary of Scottish exceptionalism though.

"I'm not sure we've got some sort of inherent or engrained rebelliousness such that you drop Burroughs on the average Scot and they're going to be any more in sympathy with it than the average Finn, say. What I might see is more the unleashing of fascism elsewhere as a reality that might bring out the thrawn in us."

Perhaps in that context the modern Scot is more open to writers like Burroughs, seeing his literary radicalism and attack on bourgeois proprieties as an attractive characteristic.

Enter Graham Rae: a bolshy, eloquent freelancer of some renown and foreword ability. His novel *Soundproof Future Scotland* is another example of a writer creating a heterotopic 22nd century nation full of exiles and reprobates. Rae first got wind of the work of William S. Burroughs through J.G. Ballard, whose work had been an obsession of Rae's after the film adaptation of his 1973 novel *Crash* came out in 1996. Ballard, who was in occasional correspondence with Rae, would enthuse about the work of Burroughs to an "idolatrous degree," describing *Naked Lunch* as "the most important and original work of fiction by an American writer since the Second World War."

As a lover of American underground culture, Rae was compelled to pick up the 1959 *tour de force*. It wasn't long before his obsession switched from Ballard to Burroughs. "*Naked Lunch* became, and still is, my favourite book. Obsession is a strand of my artistic DNA, for better or perverse. I couldn't believe what I was reading. I also couldn't understand a lot of it either."

But Rae echoes Duncan's sentiment about the international appeal of Burroughs. "I think William S. Burroughs is an inspirational enigma to many writers with an interest in 'alternative' literature and lifestyles. He's the whole devo-pervo package: wife-murderer (cos he *did* murder her; it was no accident), homosexual, pederast, trust-fund baby, slumming-it junkie 'outlaw,' internationalist, shotgun artist, occult dabbler, and general all-round fucking maniac. I think maybe, in one way, his self-destructiveness might appeal to some Scottish writers because of our self-oppression with drugs and alcohol, but I do hope that is becoming an antediluvian notion of self-and-nation-and-culture-hood and will go away. Ballard rated Burroughs and *Naked Lunch* above all, so I checked it out and became obsessed with it. I loved the fractured poetry of it, the sick humour, the decadence, the scumfuck worldview, the internationalism, the general fucked-up-ocity of it. But what I really liked was the fact I did not understand a lot of it on initial reading (outdated druggie lingo and such – Edinburgh gets a mention in there, by the way), so I had to look up stuff and read and reread to know what the fuck he was going on about. I loved that. Lovely linguistic finger-licking and learning and comprehension constant obsession classes, putting in far more fucking work towards words in general than any five dilettante English students at a university. I also liked the juxtaposition of the clear madness of Burroughs, and the deep-dish sanity of Ballard, who also had his own perverse peculiarities. They lived very similar lives, in some ways - both trained as doctors for a while, both trained in flying, both lost a wife, both wrote totally shocking writing through trauma-solution-seeking."

And we are in the midst of trauma, as Duncan reminds us, suggesting Burroughs' work is a more pertinent tonic now than ever before:

"Well, more than, you know, an American pop

culture where Orlando Jones gets fired from *American Gods* because the Black politics of defiance his character embodies is deemed too provocative, where the new *Star Wars* kowtows to straight white male fanwankery. I wouldn't be surprised to see US and UK culture get more chickenshit over the next few years. In a world we've fucked with climate change, with billionaires running grotesque puppet clowns like BawJaws or Trump, maybe Burroughs' unpeeling of the niceties down to that 'naked lunch' will feel as pointed and relevant here as the sort of left-wing avant-gardism we saw in Lorca or Jodorowsky reacting against the corrupt authoritarianism of their environs. Maybe."

In spite of all this negativity, Duncan remains optimistic that modern Scottish fiction has emerged from its post-WW2 conflation of relevance with realism.

"That sense in the wake of Modernism's elitism and even outright dalliances with fascism that fiction had to be by the people, of the people, for the people, and about the people, had to cleave to contemporary realism as per the Angry Young Man kitchen sink drama so as not to be, to put it bluntly, poncy wank. Apart from Gray and Banks, it felt like we were kinda dominated by the Kelmans and McIlvanneys for a long time, like the social conscience of writers and readers coming from working-class backgrounds fed into a wider zeitgeist that had to cast the fantastic as magic realism to take it seriously – or dismiss it to the ivory towers of postmodernism as mere gameplay – such that anything too outré had to try and find its home in the commercial genres of Soundproof Future Scotland."

Which, Duncan admits, had its own set of problems in the shape of genre conventions and commercial expectations.

"Over the last few decades, as Gen X came of age, we've seen a wholesale victory for geekdom in the culture at large, to the point of reactionary toxicity and disenchantment, people getting sick of the entitled demands for nostalgic formulaic product. The pop culture that's taken dominance and asserted the legitimacy of the strange again in its most commercial forms has become characterised by backlash upon backlash. With any luck, maybe that'll turn the audience (and the would-be creators among them) to questioning the nostalgia, the slick pandering. I'll lap up a *Marvel* movie or a *Star Wars* film as happily as anyone, to be clear, but I'd kinda like to see the death of the whole investment of identity we see in fandom, the simmering frustrations of progressives with industry conservatism translate to a thirst for fictions that just take a baseball bat to expectations."

Whether that'll happen, neither Duncan nor Rae can predict. The Glasgow Science Fiction Writers' Circle has swollen in numbers hugely over the last few years, so there's a new throng of angry young Moderns coming through the ranks. And Burroughs' influence can be felt throughout the nation's science fiction canon. Preston Grassmann, Scottish SF novelist and editor at *Locus* magazine, believes William S. Burroughs was just as indispensable to science fiction in the UK as The New Wave was to American SF.

"He was an insurrectionist, breaking down the traditional forms of genre, while revealing a more nuanced view of the world. His writing seemed to owe more to quantum physics than the literary predecessors he admired, revealing a much more elusive and multiform reality than we'd ever seen before. Writers like John Brunner, J.G. Ballard, and other experimentalists were inspired by this narrative freedom, and they went on to subvert the conventional standards of format, propriety, and style in their own way."

Ken MacLeod first read *about* Burroughs in *Bomb Culture* by Jeff Nuttall in the early seventies and took it rather more seriously than he should have:

"It's still a great individual summation of the fifties and sixties cultural upheaval – a document of its time, let's say. And there may have been some other indirect influence because Burroughs certainly had an impact on UK SF, particularly the New Wave of the sixties – whose starting point was that if SF was ever to grow up and become a worthwhile contemporary literature that faced the realities of our time and its potential futures squarely, it had to learn from or even become part of the artistic avant-garde, and to apply to itself methods of criticism more exacting than those of scientific plausibility and a jolly good read. Some of Burroughs' techniques (cut-up and other fragmented forms) and content (extreme violence, scenes of a sexual nature) may well have influenced (say) a work such as J. G. Ballard's *The Atrocity Exhibition*."

MacLeod remembers his good friend, the preeminent Iain Banks, having a copy of *Naked Lunch* and other titles on his shelves of paperbacks.

"We're talking about late secondary school and early student years here. But I don't recall him enthusing over them and pressing them on his pals to read, as he did with *Fear and Loathing in Las Vegas* and *Catch-22*. But like me he read the New Wave SF authors avidly (I've often spoken of the impact of the *New Worlds* paperback series) and unlike me he read widely in classical and contemporary literature. Perhaps the most direct echo of Burroughs in his writing is a glee in bizarrely named or motivated gangs (cliques/cults/sects) such as the Eaters in *Consider Phlebas*, the solipsist mercenaries in *Against a Dark Background*, the Interesting Times Gang (of starship AIs) in some later Culture novels."

Even *Interzone* magazine, Scotland's most cherished and lauded science fiction publication, was named after the International Zone in Tangier, Morocco, where Burroughs lived for a time. Produced by SF luminaries like John Clute, Alan Dorey, Malcolm Edwards, Colin Greenland, Graham James, Roz Kaveney, Simon Ounsley, and David Pringle, *Interzone* helped launch the careers of many important science fiction and fantasy authors, such as Michael Moorcock, Bruce Sterling, William Gibson, M. John Harrison, Stephen Baxter, Iain M. Banks, J.G. Ballard, and Harlan Ellison. While the magazine is considered a

UK publication these days (and its Scottish connections are historical and fairly tenuous at best – although head reviewer and Glaswegian, Jim Steel, remains at the magazine), *Interzone* endures as a significant piece of evidence towards our case: that Burroughs' impact on young Scottish science fiction writers and fans was pervasive. But Duncan is quick to throw a towel over the flaming stove.

"I don't see a particular slant toward the *avant-garde* amongst that wee sample of the Scottish readership, and I don't see any huge difference between the range of tastes there versus those across the wider SFF communities of the UK and US. So ultimately I'm yet to be convinced that there *is* any particular thing about the Scottish readership that Burroughs might speak to – not above and beyond the appeal of that ferocious vitality in general. I could easily be overlooking something though. It'd be nice to think we *do* have some of that fire in us as a folk."

Duncan says all this with the spirit and belief of a cultural insurgent. A man who believes that the Ancients are gone. Beside Hal Duncan and Graham Rae, their handler, a West of Scotland Mugwump sits on a bar stool draped in the butterscotch yellow of an Albion Rovers home strip, swigging from a crystal Tennent's glass half-full of warm honey with a long black giraffe tongue.

"Time to go," it mutters.

Duncan, Rae, Grassmann, MacLeod, and I observe that his eyes have surveyed too much and we watch on as he allows himself to settle into an insect calm. It seems the Mugwump is new to this part of the world, yet there is a sense he has deep roots in the surrounding clumps of soil. Blood orange suns meet outside and are immediately eclipsed by the Christ-Eye. High clouds laced with silicate particles. I'm out of time.

"Time to go."

We all leave the Interzone Pub.

Naked Punch (Redux)

Intro

At the height of my Burroughs obsession I started to write a series of short stories with him as a central character. All horribly contrived and try-hard. As a 16-year-old just turned on to all things Beat, I ran more with David Cronenberg's interpretation of Burroughs (or, more accurately, his amalgam of Burroughs and Bill Lee). The novels and poetry were beyond the simple comprehension of my teenage mind, but Burroughs *the man* fascinated me. Here was a closeted homosexual who had killed his wife, somehow got away with it, and started on a trajectory to becoming the most important American writer since Herman Melville. It was an incredible story. I wanted to write fiction about a version of him going to hell. What would happen when his time was up? What would the grim reaper say to him? What would Burroughs' version of hell look like? I started this story at 17. I was still in my final year of school and I had no fucking idea how to write properly (there's an argument that I still don't). This was my first attempt at writing something for pleasure. And it was just that. Pleasurable.

It took me two days to write and I thought it was pretty good, but it took me five years to submit it to a literary magazine. It wasn't until I was at Strathclyde University, flailing like a mad kipper on a boiling pan, that I decided to look upon writing with any degree of seriousness. I was lucky to have an inspirational lecturer in Stewart Home, who, in his own underhanded way, encouraged me to get out of uni and do what made me happy. Anything had to be better than the daily trudge of undergrad study and relentless socialising. I found the story, "Naked Punch," on an old USB. I submitted it to the online edition of *Evergreen Review*, naïvely assuming that Barney Rosset would snap up anything Burroughs-related. Imagine my smug reaction when he accepted the story! The last edition of *Evergreen Review* he would edit before his death. It did my confidence a lot of good to hear from my editor, Anjelica Young, that Rosset had enjoyed the story. I took in the balsams, the smoky ozone of Ayrshire for the first time, and felt calmed by this. Finally, I had done *something.*

It is with great sorrow that I disclose that the online version of the magazine which featured "Naked Punch" no longer exists. The story can, however, achieve a second life in this book.[38] Down the line I also published a novella called, *Last Exit to Interzone*,[39] where a time-traveller helps William S. Burroughs steal the manuscript of *Last Exit to Brooklyn* from Hubert Selby Jr. Without William S. Burroughs I wouldn't be on this road, so I guess he's to blame. The Christ-Eye sits, bloodshot and vein-streaked, like a monolith on the tallest hill eclipsing the horseshoe moonlets. With one shuddering blink it casts a solid beam of focused light onto my writhing body, setting me instantly aflame. I crumble and crack, soil pours forth from the dermis until I am reduced to a pile of reeking compost stacked next to William Lee's feet. He stares at me through the crowd with antipathy in his gaze. Everything is faintly aglow with the tangerine orange of my flames. A necessary sacrifice.

38 A version of "Naked Punch" later made an appearance in my first short story collection, Schadenfreude, published by Manchester Press, Dog Horn Publishing.
39 Also found in The Folger Variation collection.

(*Originally published in Evergreen Review #130, 2012)*

Chris Kelso

William S. Burroughs sticks his head into the toilet bowl.

– I really gotta go in there?

The dark, caped Ancient standing behind him nods to confirm. Burroughs sighs and gets back onto his knees. He hears a ticket stub wheezing like a fish out of loaves. The caped Ancient is the love of Bill's life after all, even though Killie had the best junk. Between the parted pages and weary shoulders bruised from death's grip, the dark caped Ancient is always present. He is bold printed letters on the page which outline an age-old dead belief system... That's what it always is.

Bill stares into the corroded, pebble dashed bowl. A long black junkie's turd rests half in, half out of the murky toilet water.

– Can't I at least flush this away first?

The figure shakes its head and whispers – *negative.* Sensing the figures stubborn disposition, Burroughs grips the side of the ceramic and stoops his neck down into the can.

Bill asks – Before I do this, I have to ask, is the truth true?

– Fortunately, therefore reality consists of "yes" or "no" or "god" or "not today", depending upon ourselves. Whether or not we even exist in a flat space. The holographic principle has only assured us that nothing is true, everything is true, everything and yet not even this makes sense. To others it means nothing is true in a flat space in our own universe, every conceivable action is a lie, there is no reckoning, only a license to revolt.

– Gottcha. God it smells fuckin' terrible in here!

– He gargles between mouthfuls of shit water. It's Bill's own bad luck that saw death come visiting in the middle of his weekly defecation. As inevitable as this call is, Bill never has been one to plan for an occasion.

– You think I'll fit down here?

Silence is his reply.

– Jeez, you're colder than Kerouac on ketamine, bub.

Once his head is completely in the bowl, he feels two cold, bony hands clutch at his shoulders and dunk him repeatedly. The heroin hoarded turd swishes around wildly, breaking up and smearing all over Bill Burroughs. After a few minutes of receiving his swirly, Burroughs tears his shoulders from death's grip and starts wheezing like a fish out of water. He pukes up relentless jets of toilet water and dabs away the stains from his face with a handkerchief. The water thunders as if the world has ended and has picked away what little has meaning, for he knows that we may have died in inaccessible parts of a distant world. Feeling damp and slightly less intelligent, he sees nothing but infinite chaos.

– I'd never fit down there anyway, you tyrant motherfucker.

Death indicates that the best way for him to reach the main pipe is foot first. Burroughs dually complies, removing both monk-straps and dipping his left toe into the pool of water.

– *Just squeeze through the waterway drain and into the waste pipe Bill*, Death instructed.

– Easy for you to say, you fuckin square.

The caped tyrant is always watching as Bill dips his left toe into the now. Into the now and then.

Once he had squashed himself into the narrow funnel leading into the cistern, a light appeared in the near distance. Bill headed towards it.

In-a-gadda-da-vida honey, Don'tcha know that honey, Don'tcha know that I love smoking that joint?

At the joint, the Juke Joint.

Bill's own shit gave way through the waterway drain and into a small guillotine to chop it off. Solid tarry little balls, all dark, all the sweet green icing, sweet, green icing, flowing down with us, too constipated to walk this land.

Wandering the sewers, it occurs to him that the Holographic Principle has only been observed by the more sullen primates. Maybe *that's* why he's in the sewers?

The smell of his own shit gives way to something more complex (*and nastier*) – the rank perfume of the underground. Bill slides out the pipe and lands in another puddle of gunk. Rats race each other on floating tampons and brown logs. All down the brick walls of the underground, menstrual waste seeps through the mortar. The smell is deadly feminine, a smell Bill has no real taste for. There are huge veined marble pillars that rotate, churning the sewer gunk into a blood-coloured stew. He spots a filthy syringe drift by his leg. The anthem of the Broken Boy. Bill sifts through the sewage to retrieve it in a way only a drug addict could ever commit to. There's still some junk in the cylinder, so he cleans the spike with his fingertip and shoots the needle home.

– Oh yeah, that's the spot baby...

When Burroughs withdraws the tip from the hook of his arm, a strange feeling rushes through his body. It tingles the toes of his feet before coursing up through the shin, past the knee, beyond the groin, and eventually landing on the underside of his gut with a THUD! He gives an almighty groan.

– That's some b-a-a-a-d junk, amigo...

Death indicates that the best warmth will never let you catch a breath.

After all of the lovers kissed my bony hands I clutch at his shoulders in the rain.

Day-Glo arrows point him in the direction to hell. He follows.

Like a water bug he pukes up relentless jets of bile.

– You fuckin square.

Faced with an endless number of tunnels and dark passageways, Bill rests a moment to consider his current situation. His nostrils flare as a new tide of faecal matter washes over the instep of his feet.

– What happened to good smells like the aroma of a

young Glaswegian catamite?

Continuing down the central tunnel, his foot crunches over rods of bone but he reassures himself that he is almost there. The Day-Glo arrows disappear halfway down the tunnel and he is left in total darkness.

– Hey, what's the fuckin' score, huh?

There's a vending machine illuminated under a spotlight that says – INSERT INDEX. TAKE ONE TICKET. Burroughs sticks his index into the slot and he feels a small guillotine chop it off at the joint. A ticket stub spits out the bottom of the machine. Bill stems the bleeding with a used-condom sheath that happens to be floating by and collects his ticket.

It says – *INTERZONE/ONE WAY/NOVA.*

A train toots its horn from somewhere inside the darkened tunnel.

– Guess I better get moving.

The ticket suddenly explodes into a million fragments in his hand. A voice from a Tannoy declares

- LAST CALL FOR NOVA EXPRESS TO INTERZONE, PLATFORM 23!

– That's my ride!

As he runs to the train door without a ticket, the engines fire into life and Bill can only watch as his ride disappears into darkness.

– I missed my train!

– Not to worry Mr. Lee, please come this way.

A tall, good looking man wearing a doctor's lab coat over bloody scrubs waves him over to a hole in the wall.

– Just pop your head in there, Mr. Lee. Please take of the toilet water and drink deep.

– I don't think so pal. Look what happened last time I stuck a part of myself into a random hole!

Burroughs un-wraps the latex Band-Aid and shakes his finger stump in the doc's face.

– My, my...

– Yeah, exactly! He is better than our Sun that exploded is a statement that still holds objectivity.

The hole in the wall looks kind of like a gaping asshole, with the off-pink subway walls and the cracked tiles around the precipice. Burroughs puts one leg into the hole. He turns to the helpful doc and says

– You look familiar.

– I don't think so. I never forget a face. That which rewards our natural behaviours produces the universe. Results obtained by many other animals have exploded as supernovae at the euphoric effects sought.

The doc smiles sinisterly and pushes the rest of Bill Burroughs into the crack...

I think to myself that I will read what I wrote before bed last night. The page is always blank....nothing.

Next to the typewriter is a big mound of white powder and beside it, a note written in a delicate script on the back of a prescription.

Bill,
Dr. Benway called. Sorry I had to leave so soon. Enjoy the Bug Powder, it's the good stuff. Don't ever forget Bill, Man is a bad animal.
Love,
Brion

Brion always had the best junk.

Afterword

Steve Finbow

Rather like the Sex Pistols gig at Manchester's Lesser Free Trade Hall on 4 June, 1976, everyone seems to have been there — for Howard Devoto, Pete Shelley, Mark E, Smith, Tony Wilson, and Stephen Morrissey read Graham Rae, Ewan Morrison, Hal Duncan, Ken MacLeod, and Christopher Kelso. William S. Burroughs was and is the man who changed their world, who put the punk in punctum—"punctum—an object or image that jumps out at the viewer within a photograph, 'that accident which pricks me but also bruises me, is poignant to me.' Punctum can exist alongside studium, but disturbs it, creating an 'element which rises from the scene' and unintentionally fills the whole image. Punctum is the rare detail that attracts you to an image, Barthes says, 'its mere presence changes my reading.'" Burroughs' presence changes lives.

Kelso maps the formative effects of Burroughs on Scottish writing, charts the hypodermic surge of the cut-up in Alba, adumbrates the experimental literary addiction in Caledonia. But what he also does is situate Burroughs as a writer of the heterotopia, of the temporary autonomous zone, the artist on the edge, the borderlands — Interzone. From Alexander Trocchi to Kelso himself, Burroughs' work infects and infests their writing with a viral experimentation, a gunfighter's fast-draw prose, the willingness to go one step further, take a risk, go out on a limb, to limn the liminal. It was Hakim Bey who said, "We're not touting the TAZ (Temporary Autonomous Zone) as an exclusive end in itself, replacing all other forms of organization, tactics, and goals. We recommend it because it can provide the quality of enhancement associated with the uprising without necessarily leading to violence and martyrdom."

Violence as methodology, violence as anti-state, as anti-power, anti-control, the violence of smithereened syntax, of spasmodic narrative. Kelso incorporates Burroughs' style as he investigates his importance. Burroughs' writing is "like an uprising which does not engage directly with the State, a guerrilla operation which liberates an area (of land, of time, of imagination) and then dissolves itself to re-form elsewhere/elsewhen, before the State can crush it." There is a guerrilla-like rebellious streak in Scottish writing — Trocchi again, Alasdair Gray,

James Kelman, Irvine Welsh — Kevin Williamson and the whole Rebel Inc. gang's Fuck the Mainstream! "Because the State is concerned primarily with Simulation rather than substance, Burroughs can 'occupy' these areas clandestinely and carry on his festal purposes for quite a while in relative peace. Perhaps Burroughs has lasted whole lifetimes because he went unnoticed—*el hombre invisible*—because he never intersected with the Spectacle, never appeared outside that real life which is invisible to the agents of Simulation."

And Kelso portrays Scotland as an oppressed heterotopia, a suppressed temporary autonomous zone, dreaming to be "a liberated area of land, time or imagination where one can be for something, not just against, and where new ways of being human together can be explored and experimented with. Locating itself in the cracks and fault lines in the global grid of control and alienation." Scotland, through the influence of the writing of William S. Burroughs, wants the fix of "an eruption of free culture where life is experienced at maximum intensity. It should feel like an exceptional party where for a brief moment our desires are made manifest and we all become the creators of the art of everyday life." Kelso shows how Burroughs' work creates "a place where people might slip into different identities, assume new ways of being and relating, become fluid and wild in ways that are constrained on the surface."

Thirteen years before the Edinburgh Writers' Conference and six months before Johnny Rotten sang, "I don't mind the things that you say / I don't even mind going out of my way / I try and do these things for you / Why should I do it I'm always untrue / Well, I did you no wrong / I did you no wrong / Going out of my head," Michel Foucault gave a lecture on "Infantile Sexuality" at the Schizo-Culture Conference organized by Semiotext(e) at Columbia University. This was an early draft of his *History of Sexuality*, and also present during the conference were Gilles Deleuze, Félix Guattari, R. D. Laing, and Burroughs. Burroughs' works can be seen as the blueprints for Foucault's heterotopias; they "are disturbing, probably because they secretly undermine language, because they make it impossible to name this *and* that, because they shatter or tangle common names, because they destroy 'syntax' in advance, and not only the syntax with which we construct sentences but also that less apparent syntax which causes words and things (next to and also opposite one another) to 'hold together'. Heterotopias (such as those to be found so often in Borges [and Burroughs]) desiccate speech, stop words in their tracks, contest the very possibility of grammar at its source; they dissolve our myths and sterilize the lyricism of our sentences."

Burroughs & Scotland reflects on the *Naked Lunch* author's physical and psychic presence in the lives of Scottish writers and artists. In Deleuze's book on Foucault, he writes, "This modern literature uncovers a 'strange language within language' and, through an unlimited number of superimposed grammatical constructions, tends towards an atypical form of expression that marks the end of language as such (here we may cite such examples as Mallarme's book, Peguy's repetitions, Artaud's breaths, the agrammaticality of Cummings, Burroughs and his cut-ups and fold-ins, as well as Roussel's proliferations, Brisset's derivations, Dada collage, and so on). And is this unlimited finity or superfold not what Nietzsche had already designated with the name of eternal return?" Kelso charts the eternal return of Burroughs in the writings of Trocchi, Iain Banks, Irvine Welsh, Ken McLeod, Ewan Morrison, and Hal Duncan. He channels these writers, while synchronously crafting an ectoplasmic prose of his own and in this he diagnoses the contagion of Burroughs, the effects of his writing, the centrality of heroin and drugs within his methodology, and the perspicacity and prescience of his philosophy.

In an interview with Jean Baudrillard, Sylvère Lotringer, the organiser of the Schizo-Culture Conference, writes, "Every time I meet William Burroughs, I feel I'm in the presence of a feisty corpse. As a living person he seems rather bored. I asked him if he would go to the moon. 'Of course,' he replied. 'I'd go anywhere; I'd leave the solar system if they came to get me in a flying saucer.' 'Even if there is no coming back?' I asked. He looked at me. 'Why come back?'"

Kelso, in writing *Burroughs & Scotland*, reanimates Burroughs' corpse, reincarnates Burroughs in the corps of contemporary Scottish writers, and contributes new and pertinent knowledge to the Burroughs corpus.

Notes

Page 2 – Diane Loxley, The Pure Story of 'Treasure Island', in Children's Literature Classic Texts and Contemporary Tends, Milton Keynes/London, A&C Black in association with the Open University, 2009, p.65

Page 11 - Ted Morgan, Literary Outlaw, W. W. Norton & Company, 1988, p. 334.

Page 14 - Ted Morgan, Literary Outlaw, W. W. Norton & Company, 1988, p.332.

Page 14 - Alan Campbell and Tim Niel A Life in Pieces: Reflections on Alexander Trocchi, Rebel Inc, 1997, p.55

Page 16 - Cosmonaut of Inner Space: An Existential Enquiry into the Writing of Alexander Trocchi, 2015, p.3

Page 17 - Ted Morgan, Literary Outlaw, W. W. Norton & Company, 1988, p.400

Page 23 - Transatlantic Review (#11 – Winter), 1962,

p.34
Page 23 - J. Michael Lennon: Norman Mailer: A Double Life, Simon & Schuster, 2014, P. 313
Page 26 - Myra Cohn Livingston, Poetry: Why and How?, John Hopkins University, 1980, p.17
Page 27 - Dr Stewart Smith, Edinburgh Little Magazines, Newcastle University, 2010, p.1
Page 30 - James Campbell, On the Trail of Trocchi, Scottish Review of Books, 2018
Page 33 - Gambit: Edinburgh University Review (Autumn), 1962, p. 34
Page 34 - Bill Morgan, Rub Out the Words, The Letters of William S. Burroughs, Harper Collins, 2012, p.334
Page 43 – Alexander Trocchi, Man of Leisure, Alma Classics, 2019, p.2
Page 48 - Daniel Odier, The Job: Interviews with William S. Burroughs, Grove Press, 1970, p. 200
Page 50 - L. Ron Hubbard, Dianetics: The Modern Science of Mental Health, 1950, p.178
Page 51, Paulette Cooper, The Scandal of Scientology, Tower Publications, 1971, p.30
Page 54 - William S. Burroughs, Ali's Smile, Expanded Media Editions, 1071, p.45

Made in the USA
Middletown, DE
06 April 2021

37041537R00076